The Joy of Family

The Joy of Family

R

A Rutledge Book
The C. R. Gibson Company
Norwalk, Connecticut
U.S.A.

Library of Congress Catalog Card Number 69-17718
SBN 8378-1856-7
Prepared and Produced by Rutledge Books, Inc.
Copyright © MCMLXIX by The C. R. Gibson Company
Norwalk, Connecticut, U.S.A.
All rights reserved

We are not born as the partridge in the wood,
or the ostrich of the desert, to be scattered everywhere;
but we are to be grouped together, and brooded
by love, and reared day by day in that first of
churches, the family.

Henry Ward Beecher

Perhaps the greatest blessing in marriage is that it lasts so long. The years, like the varying interests of each year, combine to buttress and enrich each other.

Richard C. Cabot

Marriage resembles a pair of shears, so joined that they cannot be separated: often moving in opposite directions, yet always punishing any one who comes between them.

Sydney Smith

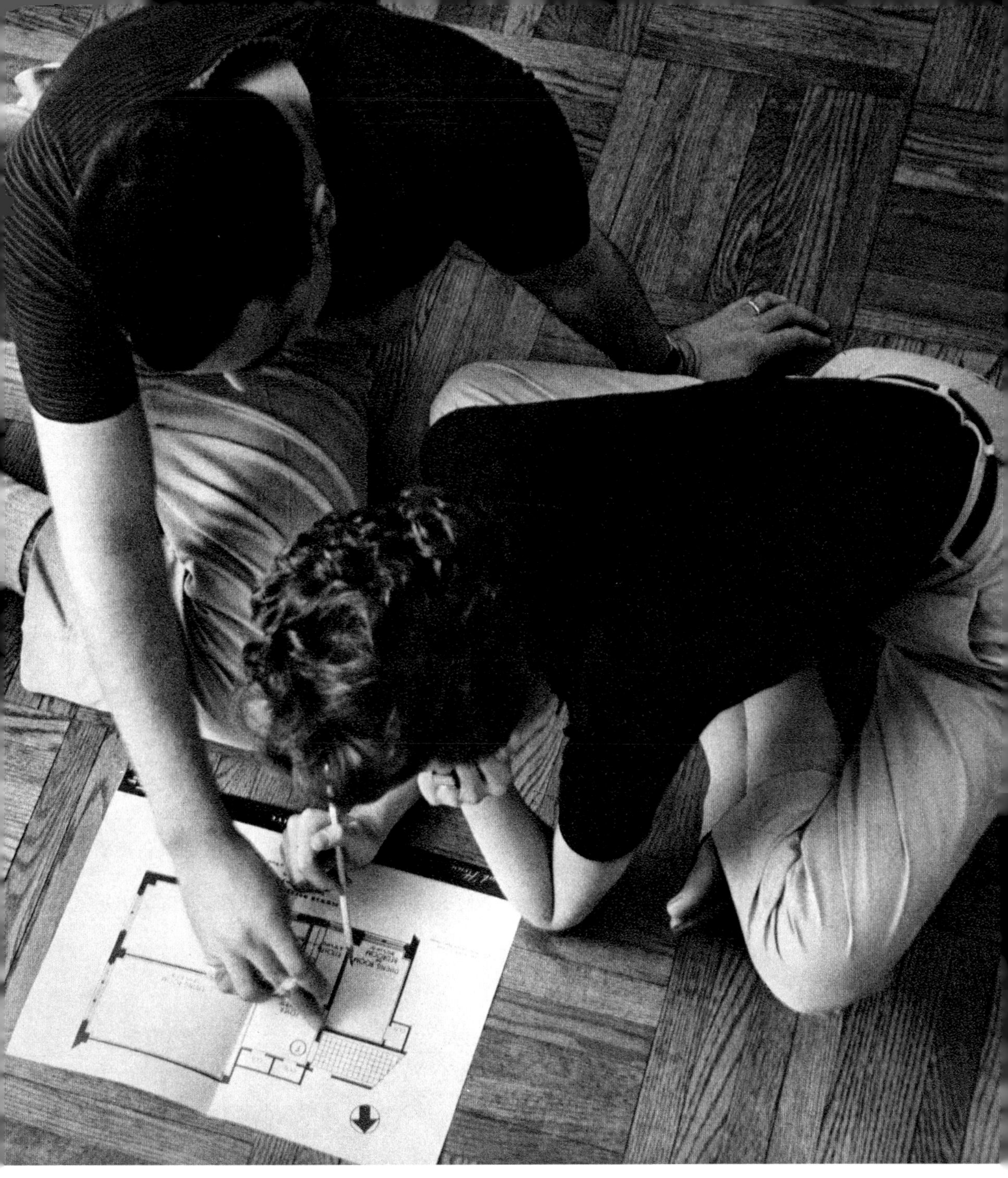

... not a union merely between two creatures ... the intention of that bond is to perfect the nature of both, by supplementing their deficiencies with the force of contrast, giving to each sex those excellences in which it is naturally deficient ...

Frederick William Robertson

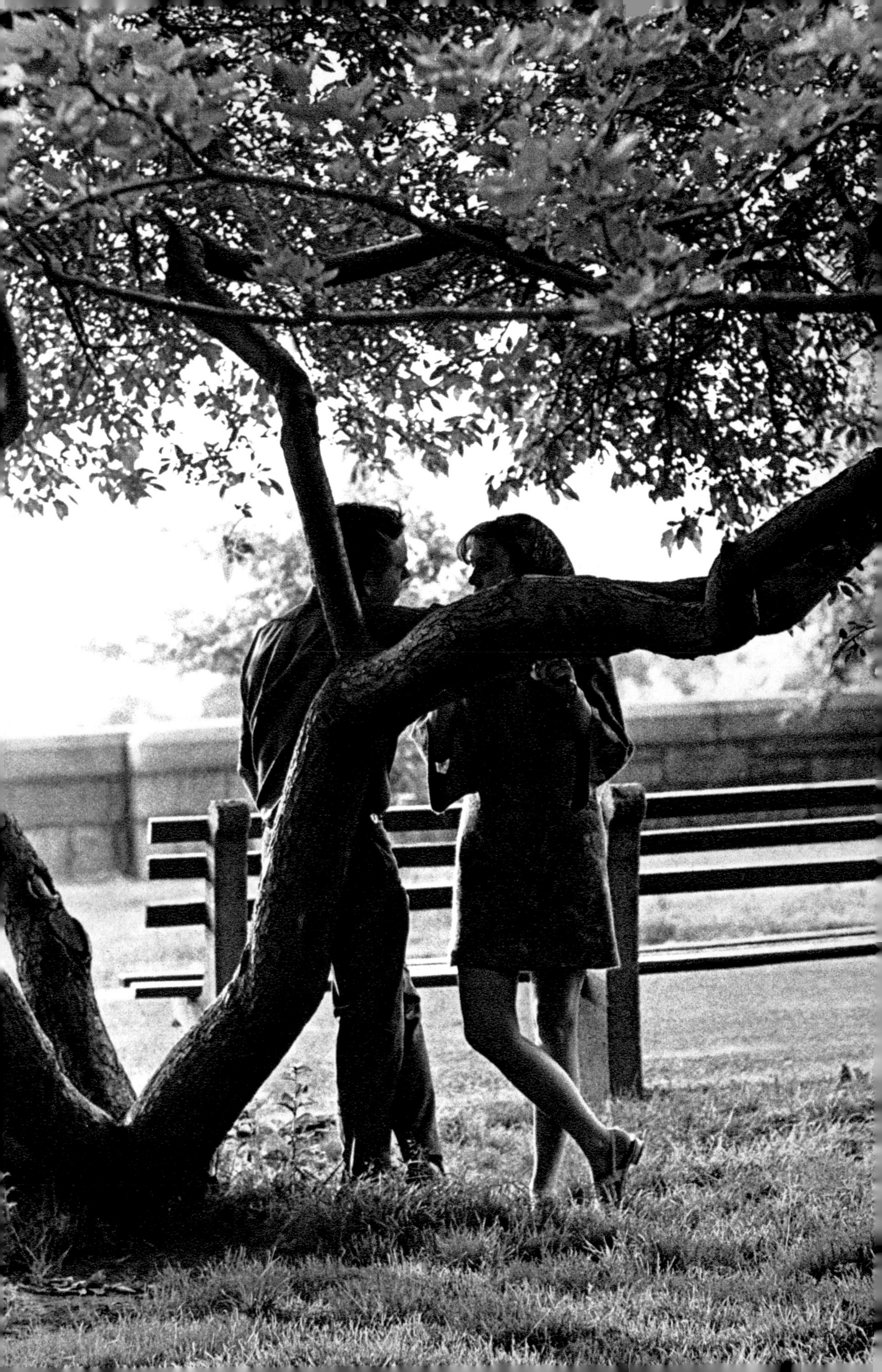

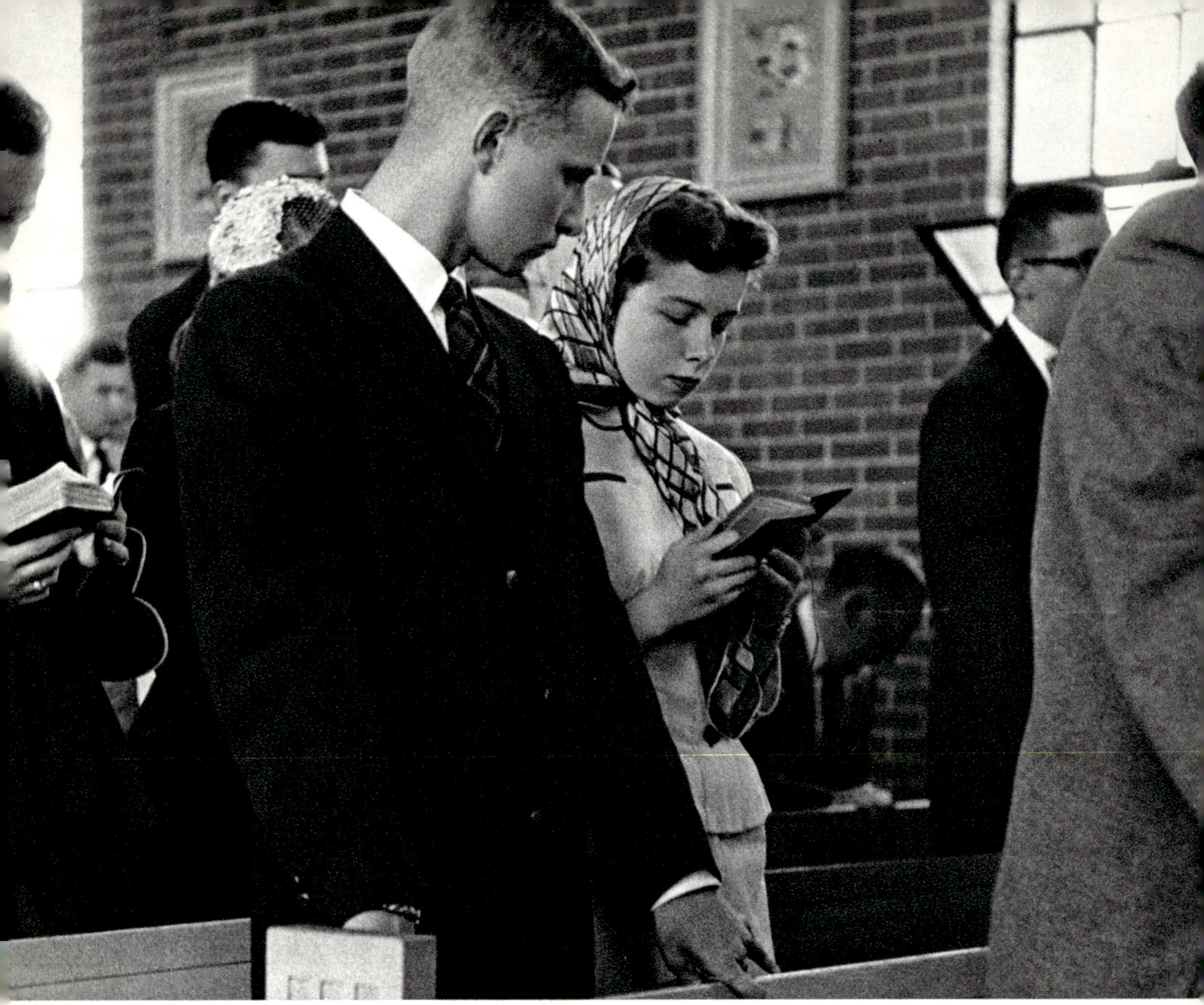

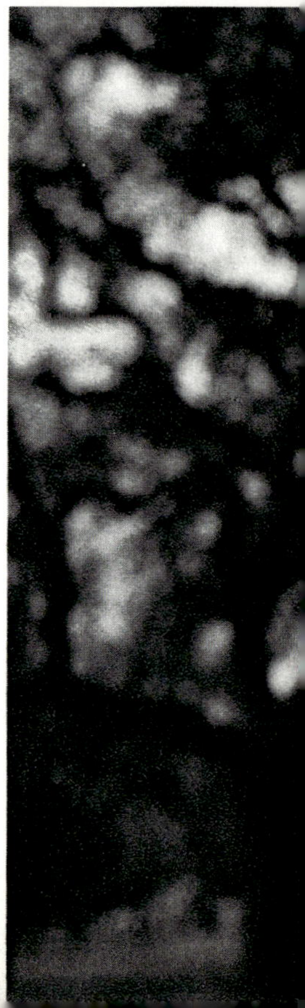

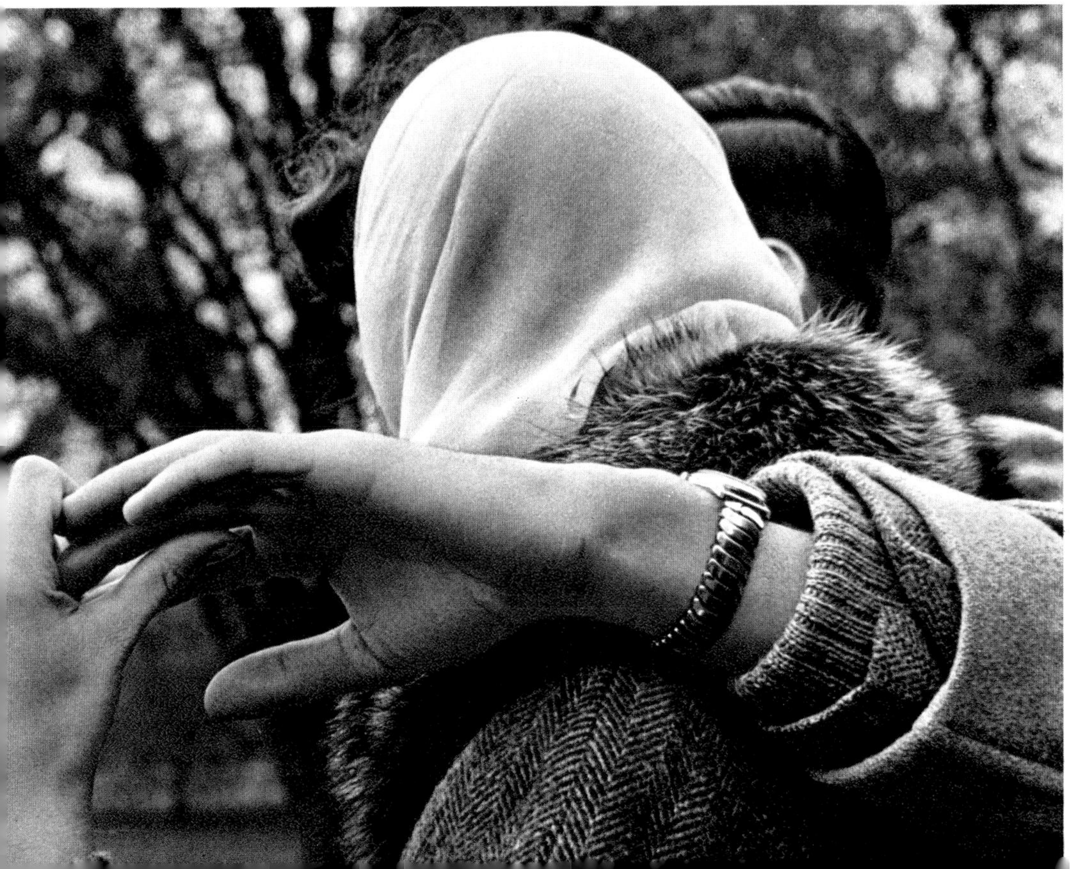

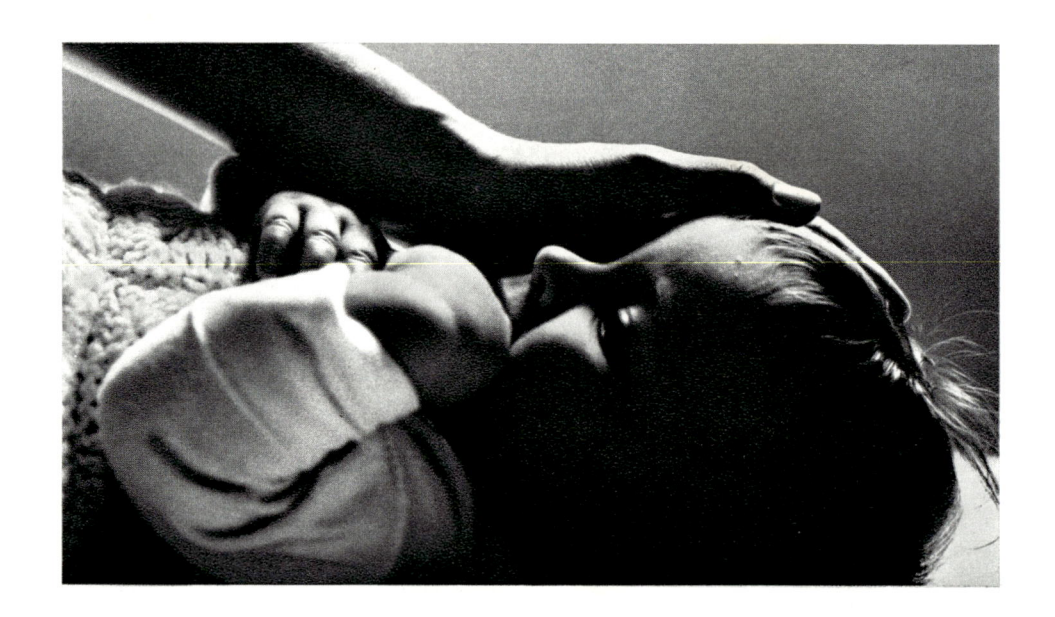

Dependence is a perpetual call upon humanity, and a greater incitement to tenderness and pity than any other motive whatever.

William Makepeace Thackeray

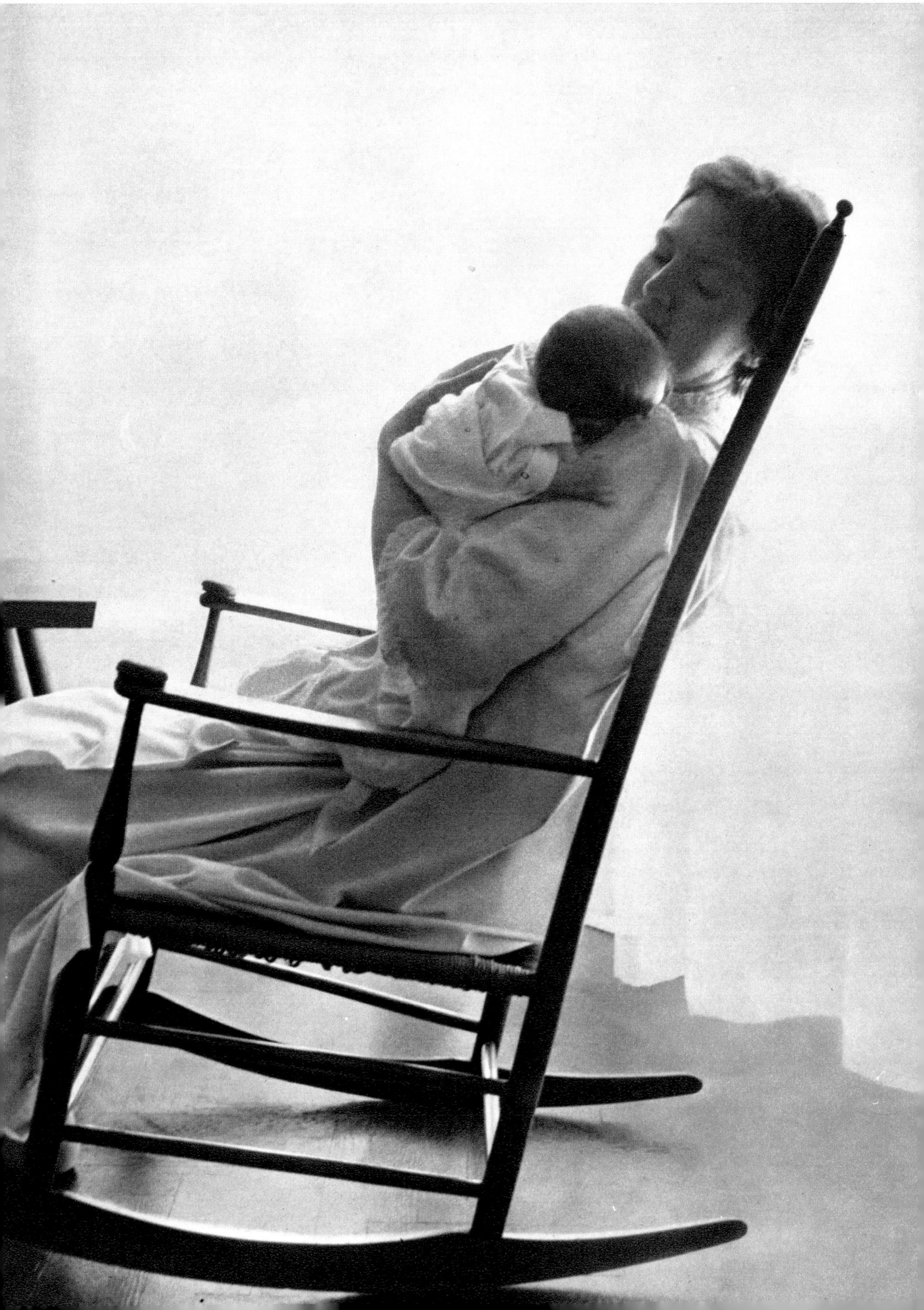

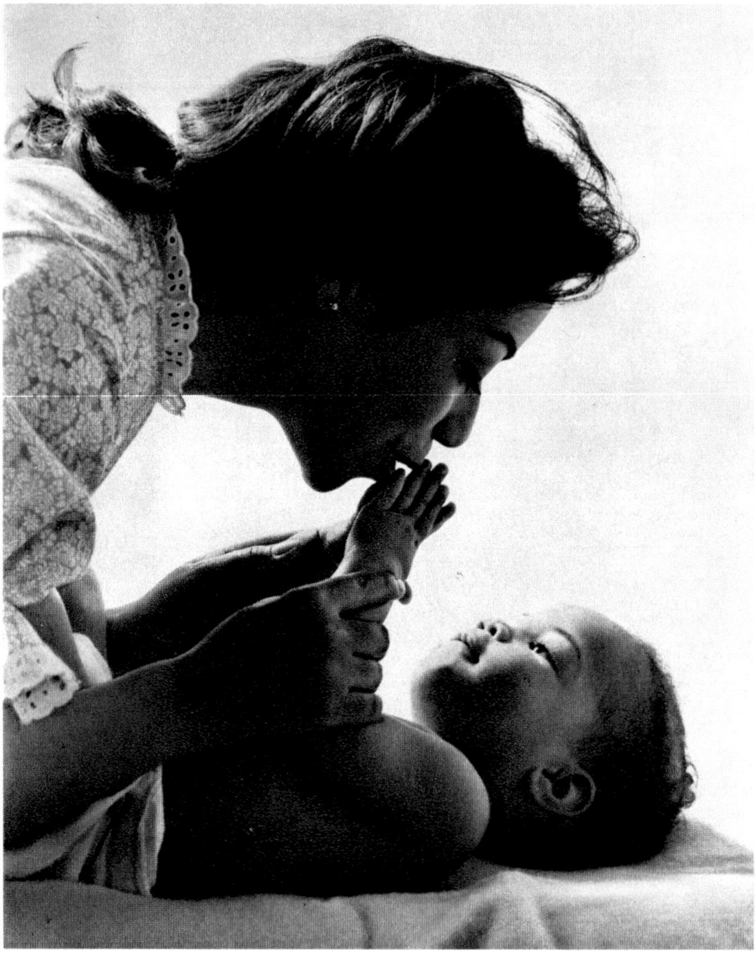

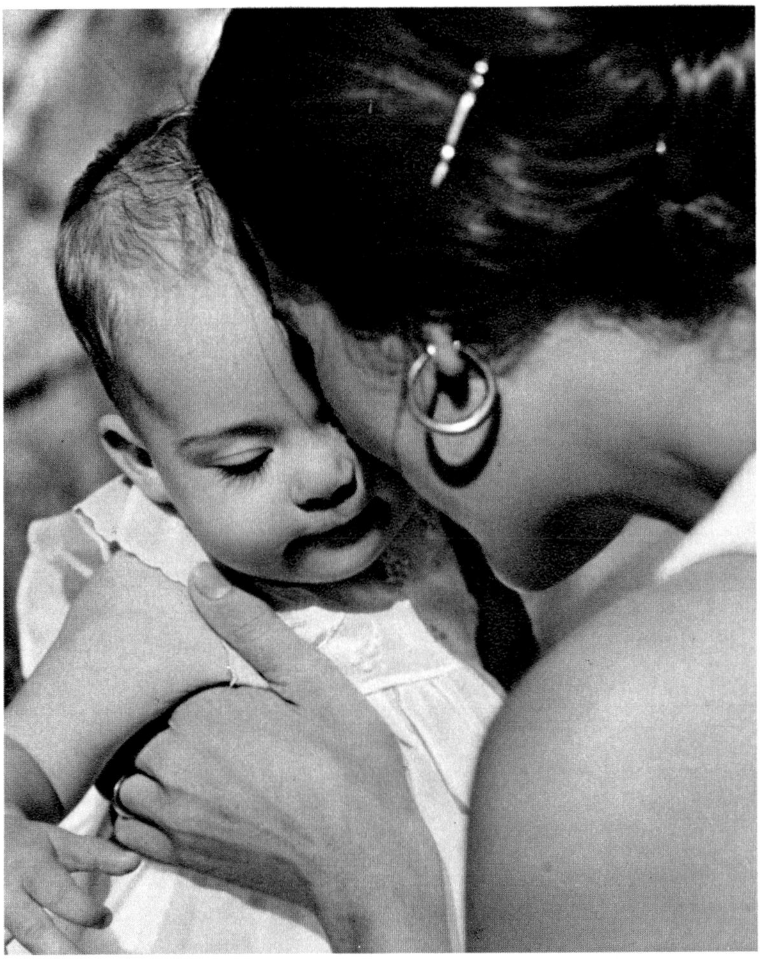

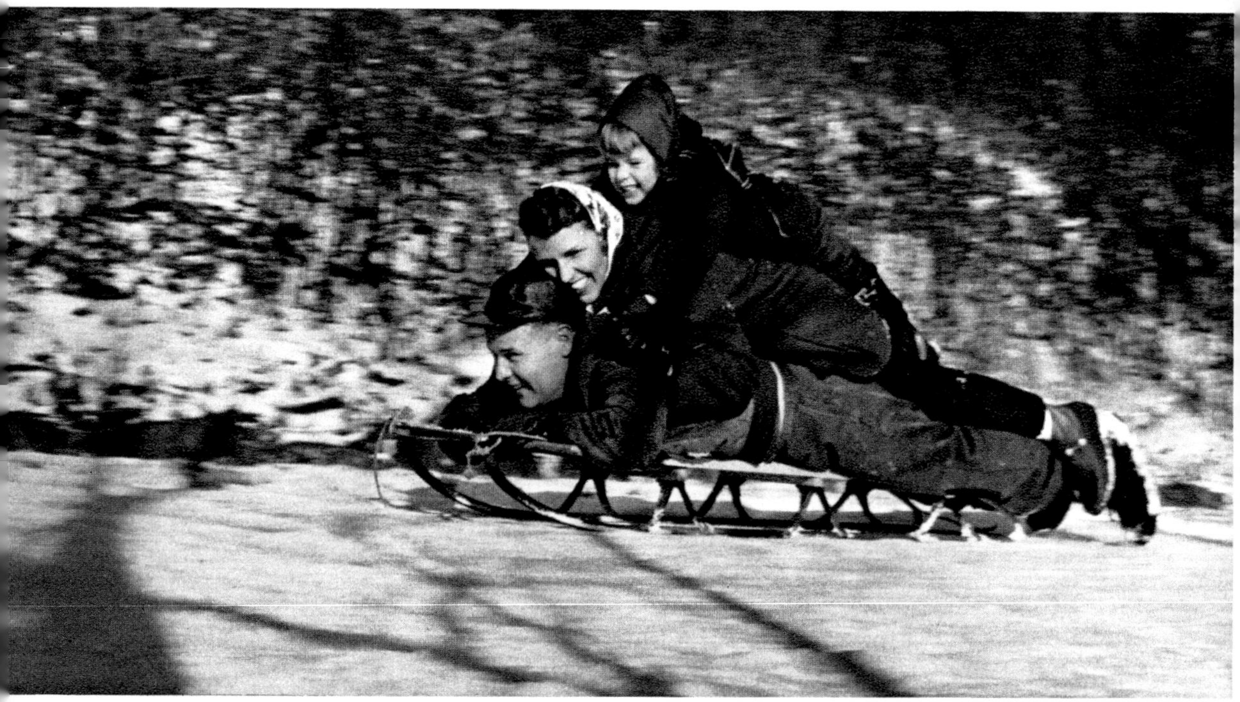

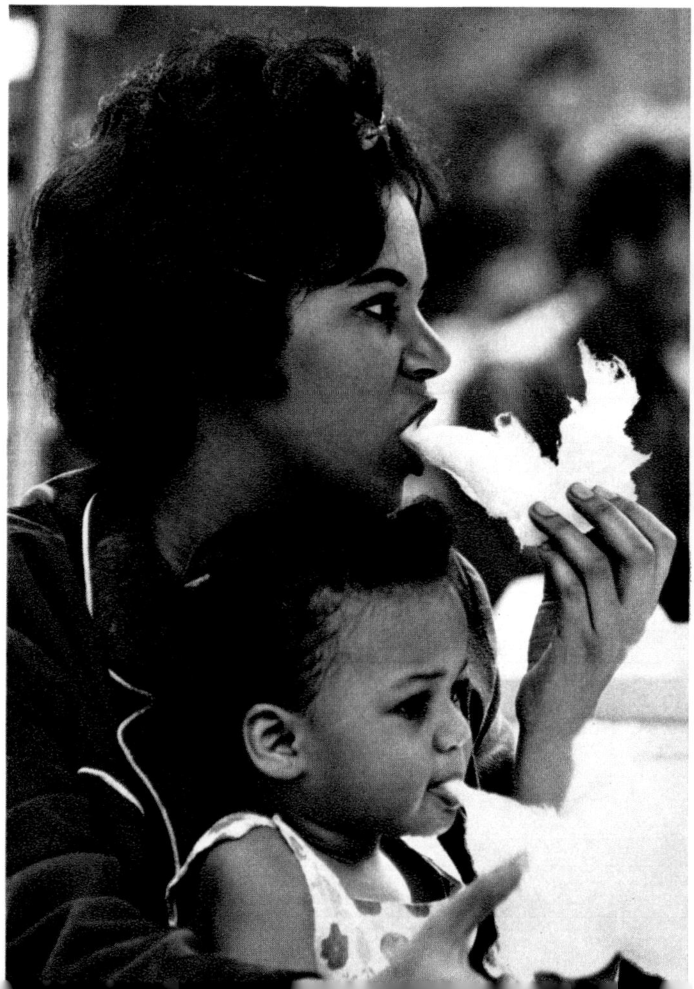

Better to be driven out from among men than to be disliked of children.

Richard Henry Dana

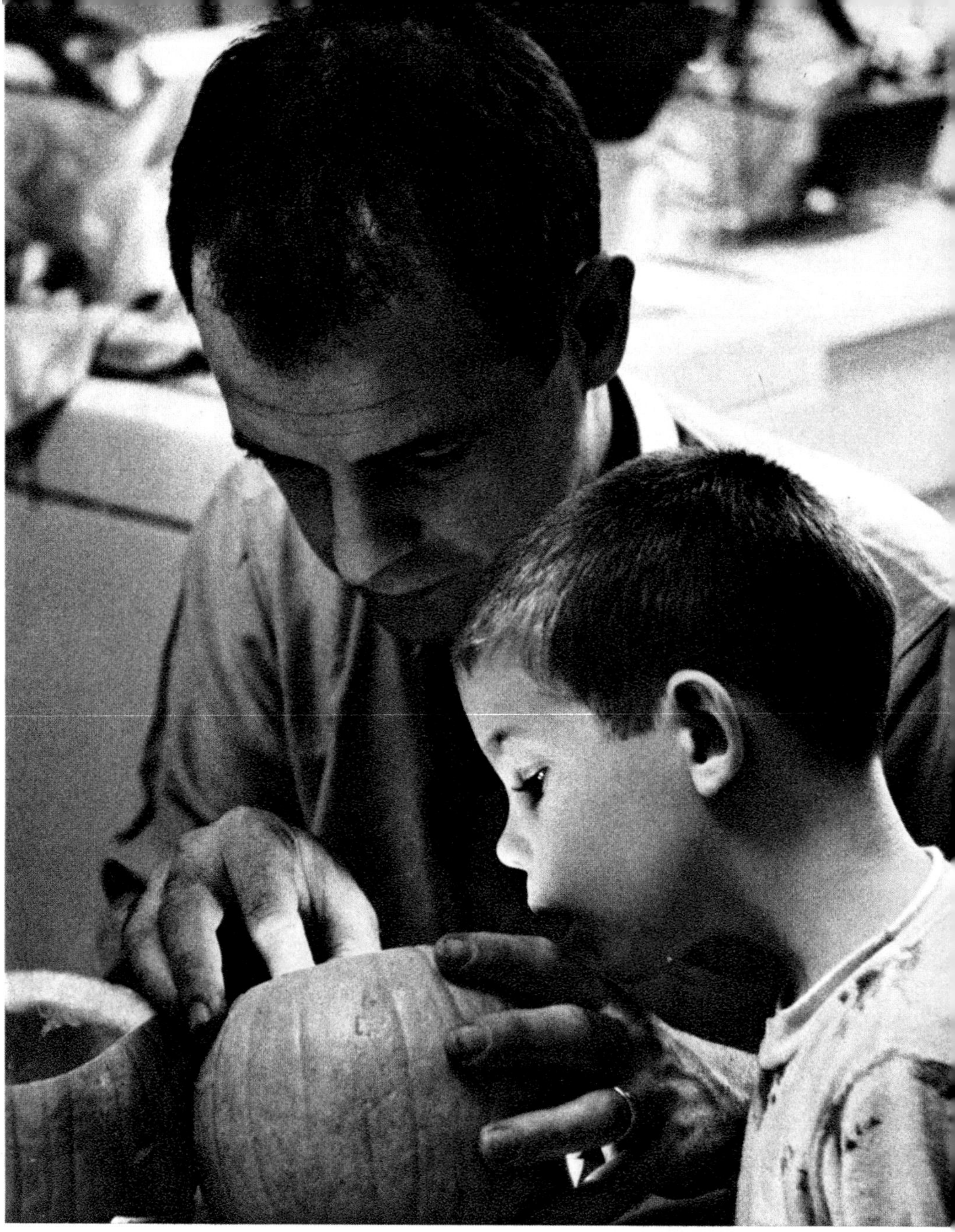

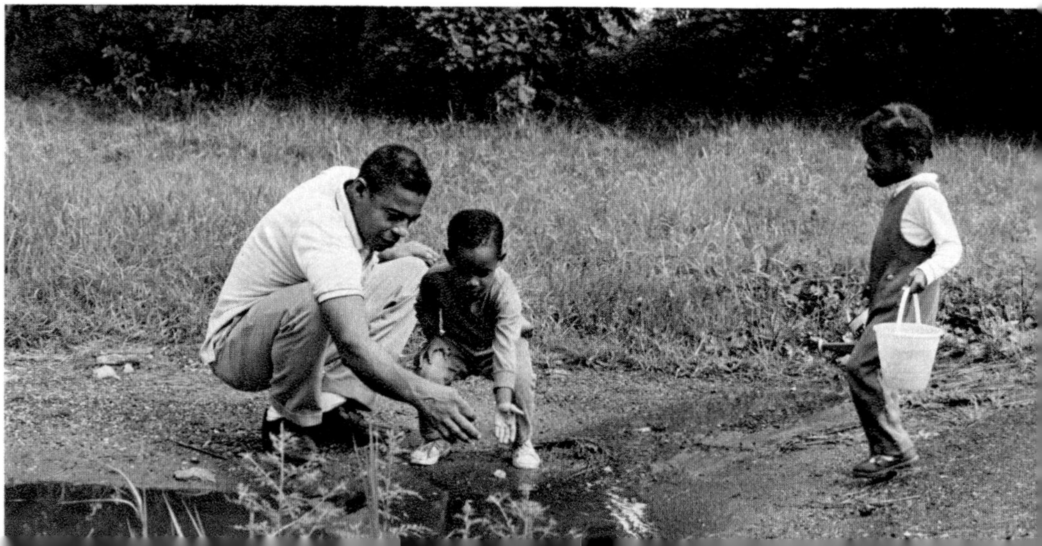

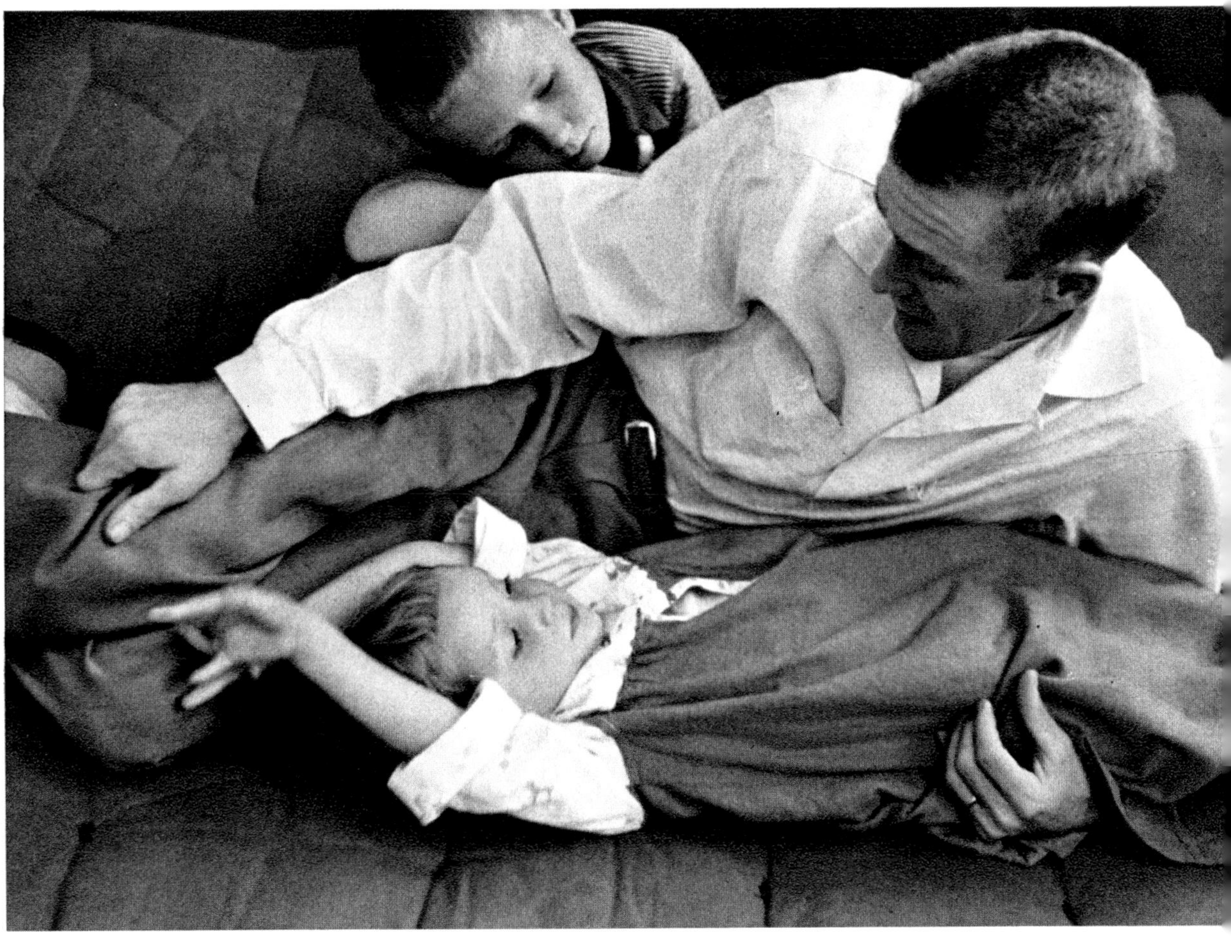

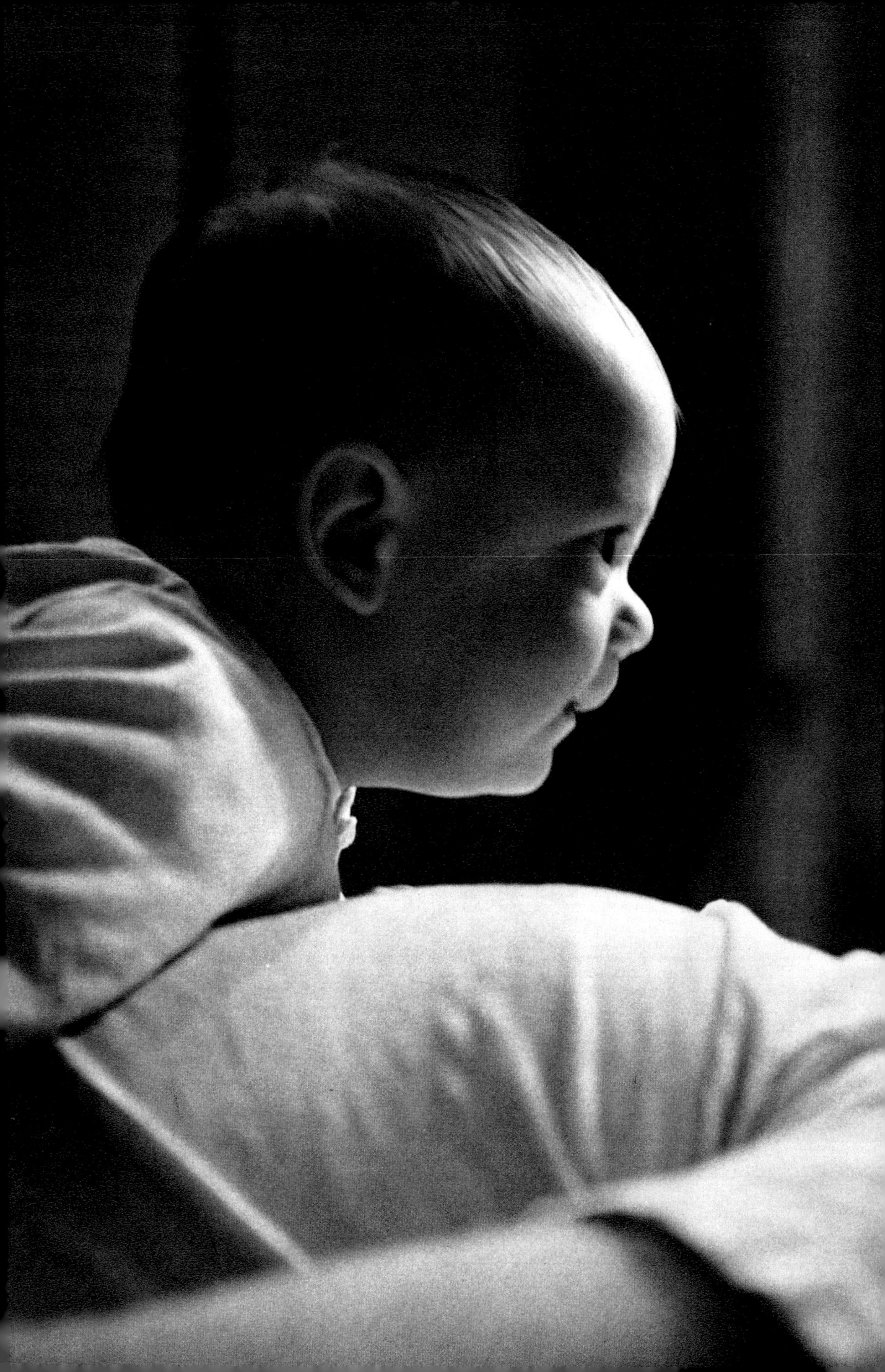

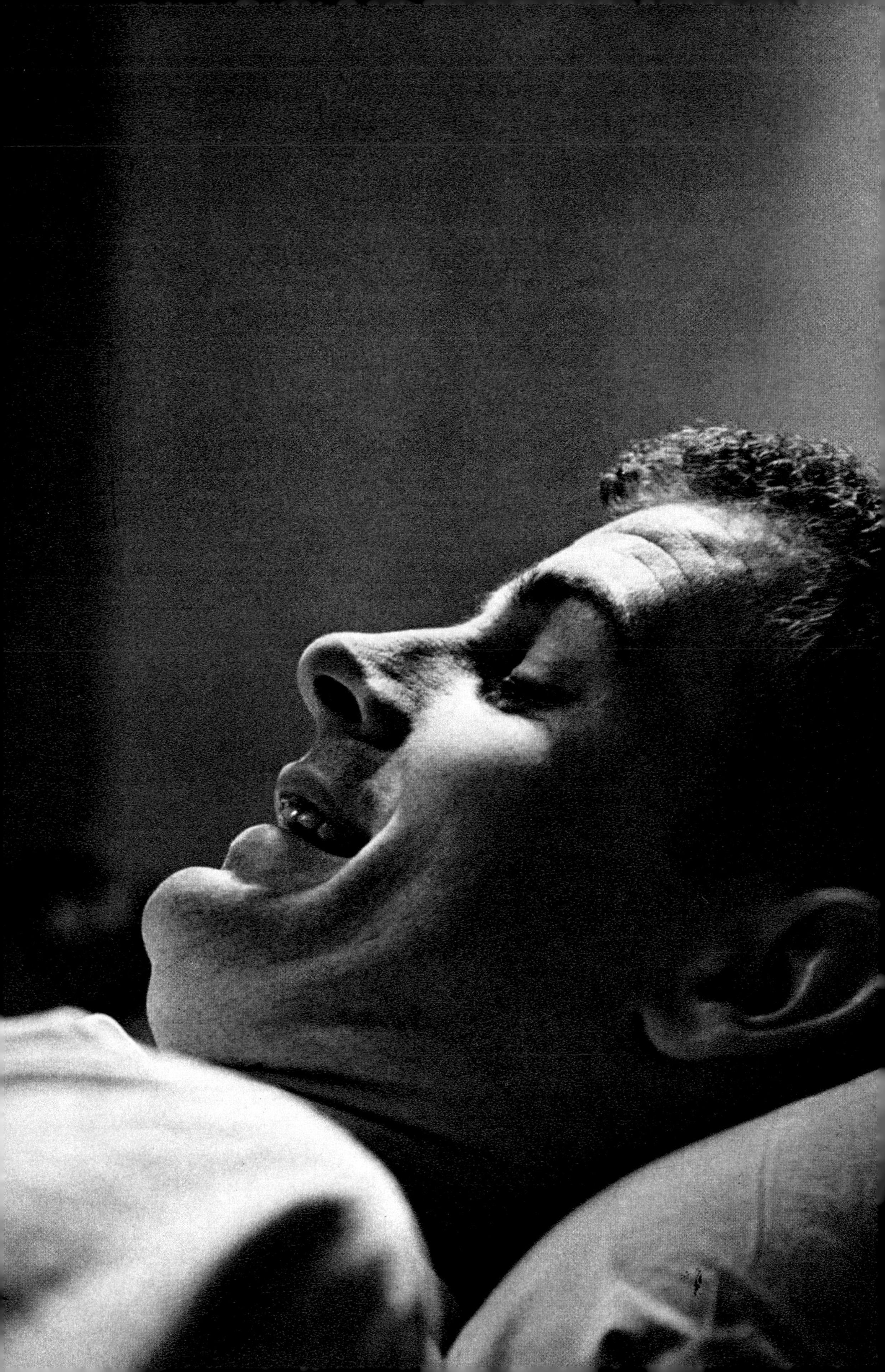

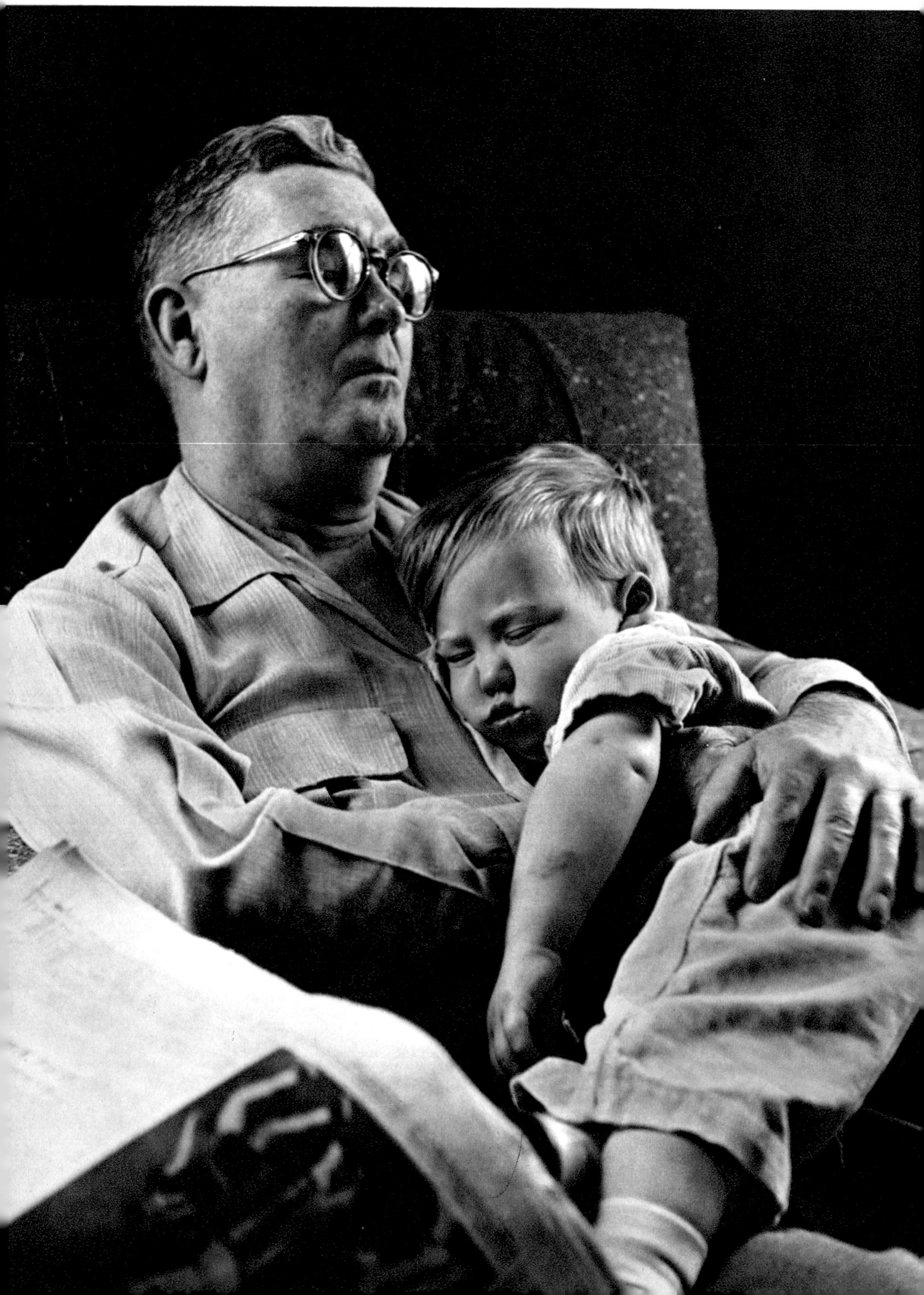

Ye are better than all the ballads
    That ever were sung or said;
For ye are the living poems
    And all the rest are dead.

Henry Wadsworth Longfellow

I have often thought what a melancholy
world this would be without children; and
what an inhuman world, without the aged.

Samuel Taylor Coleridge

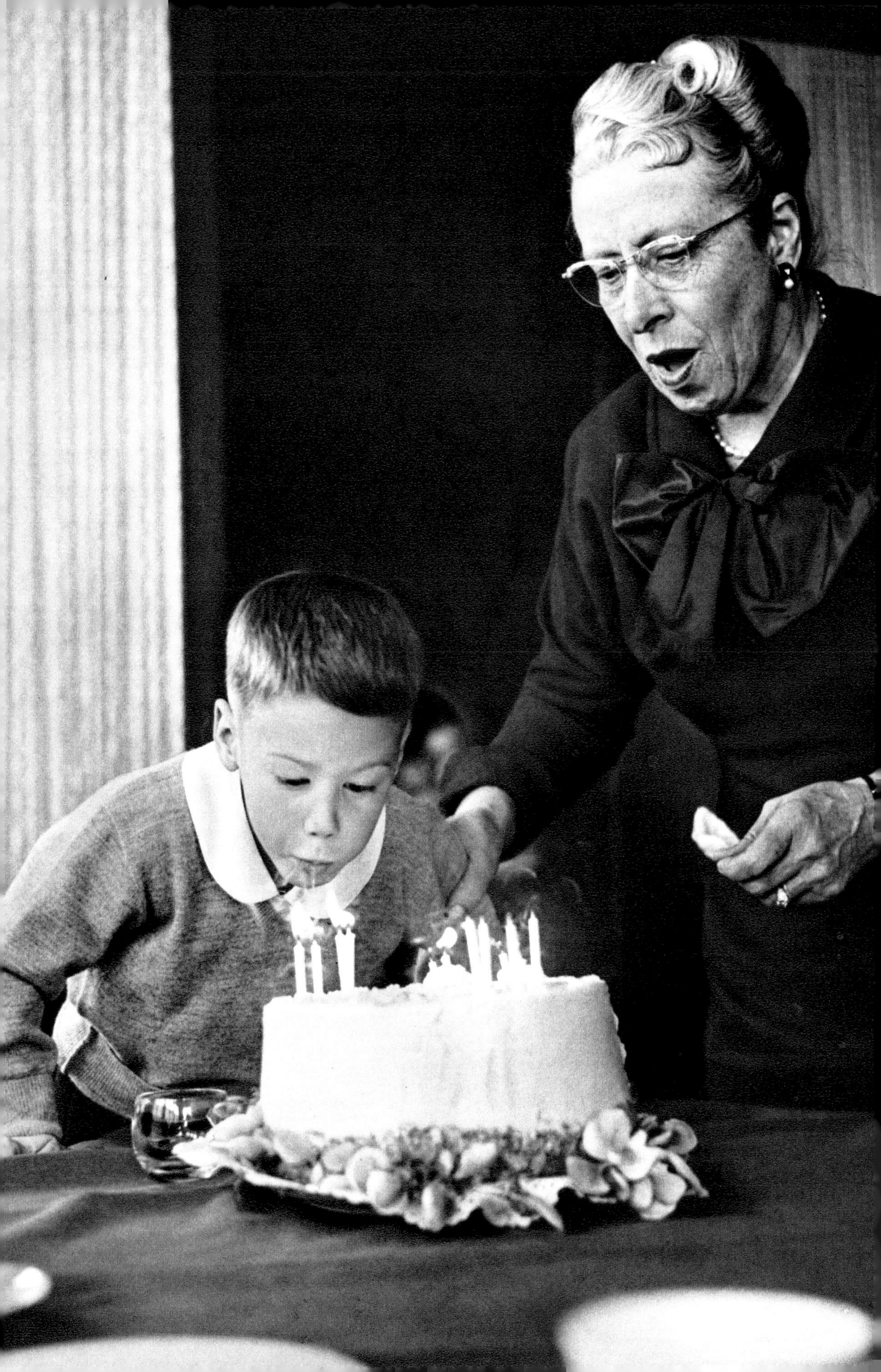

So nigh is grandeur to our dust,
    So near is God to man,
When Duty whispers low, *Thou must,*
    The youth replies, *I can.*

Ralph Waldo Emerson

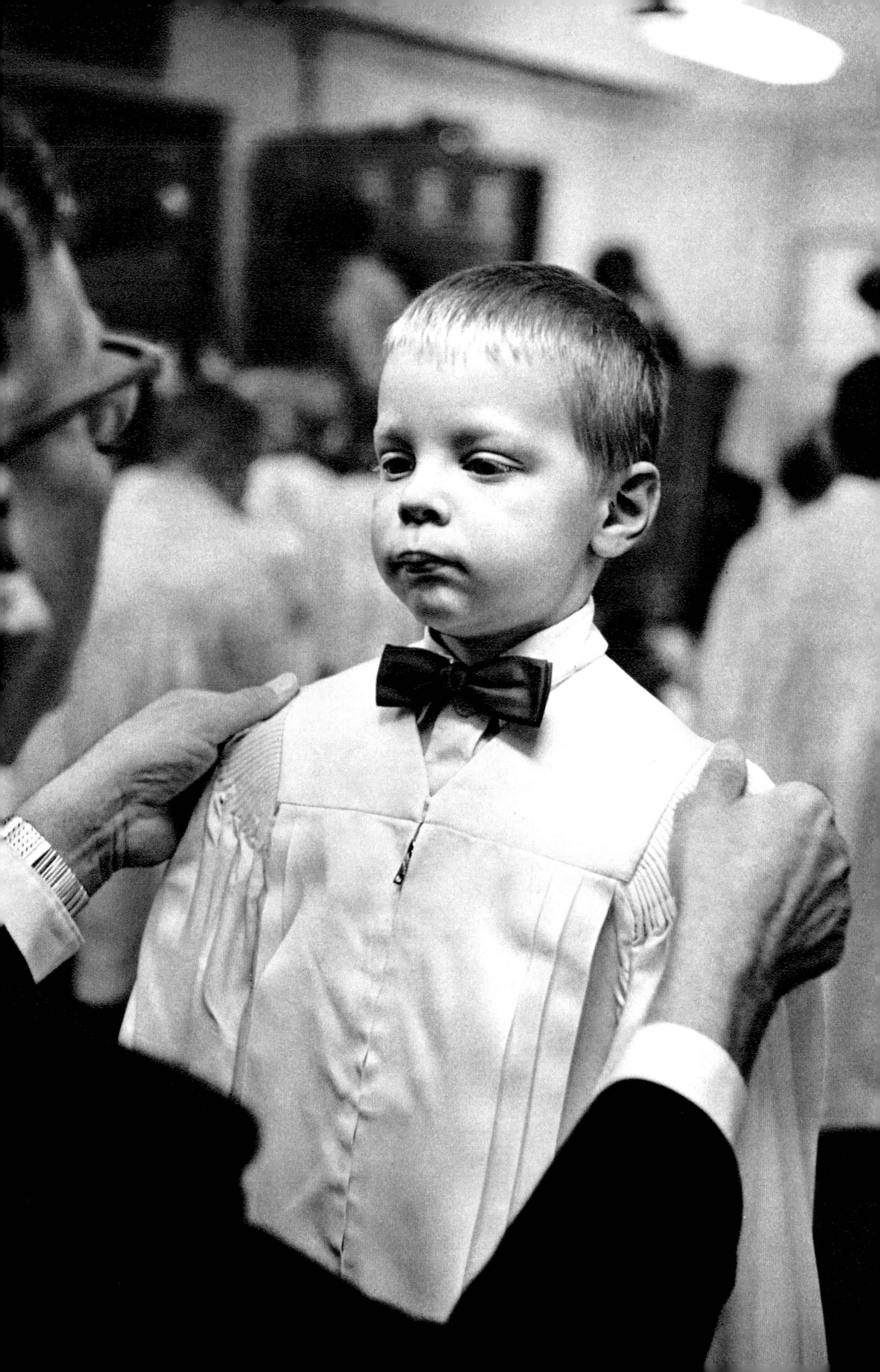

Her children rise up and call her blessed.

Proverbs 31:28

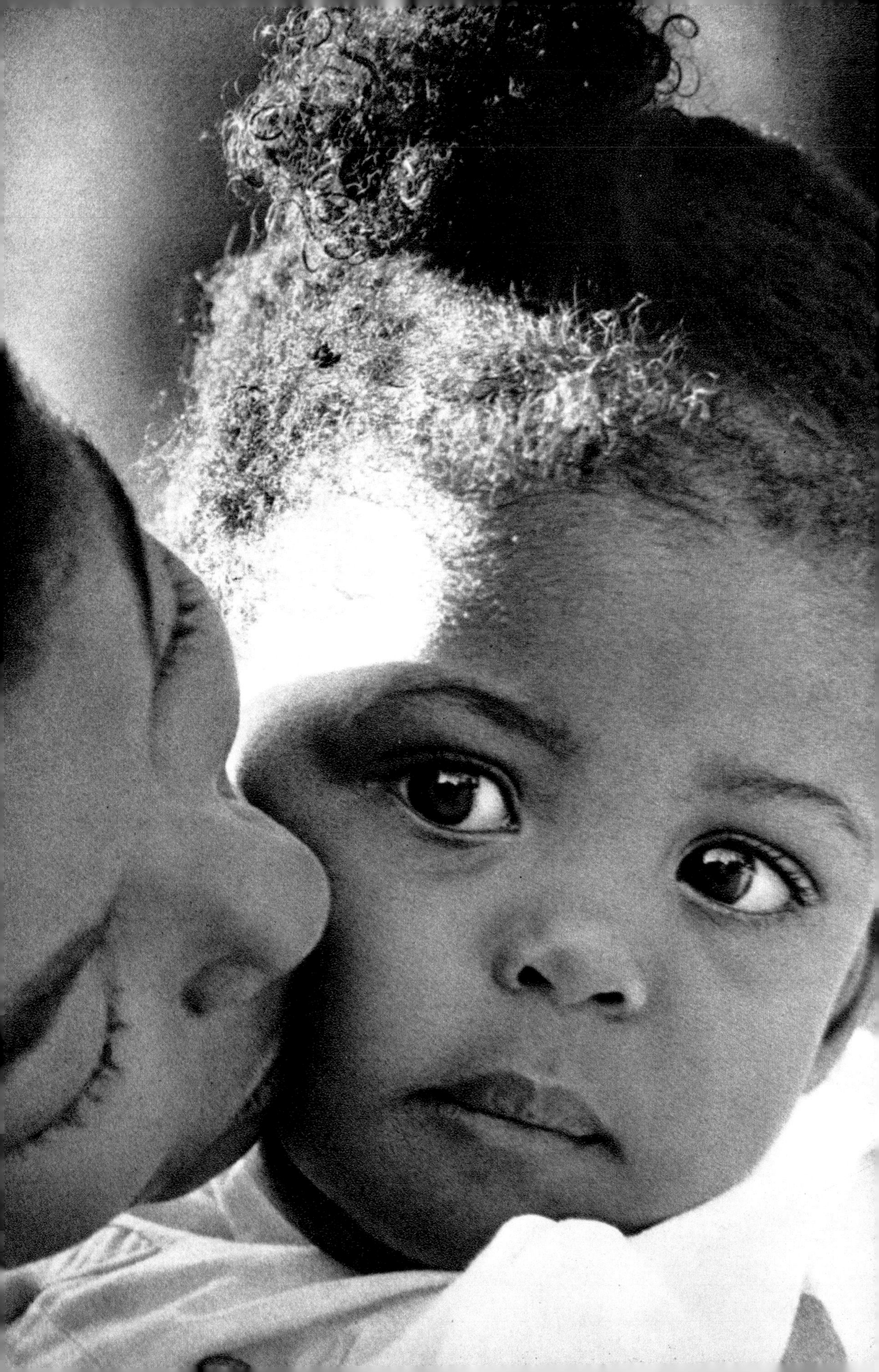

I love these little people; and it is not a slight thing when they, who are so fresh from God, love us.

Charles Dickens

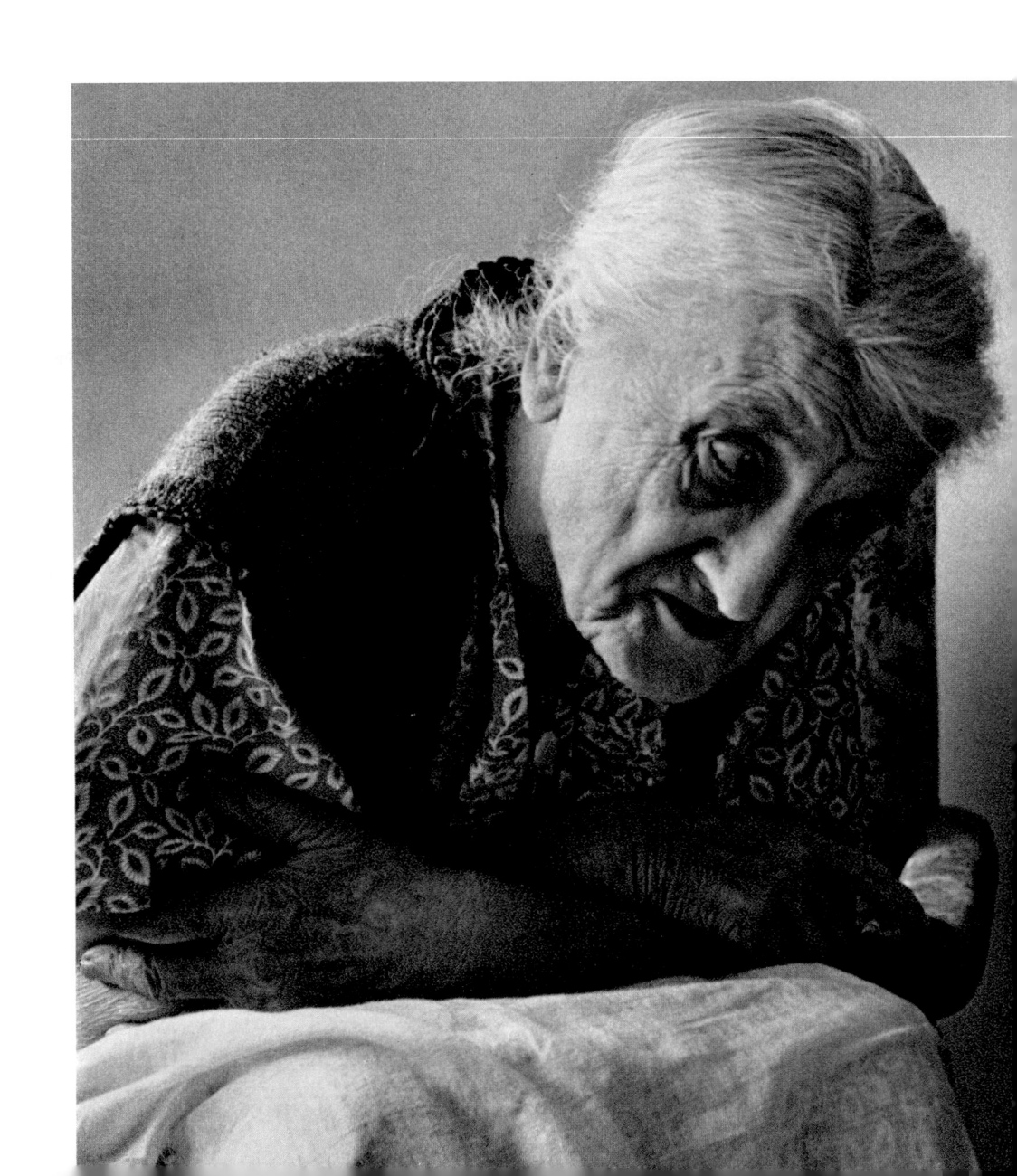

33

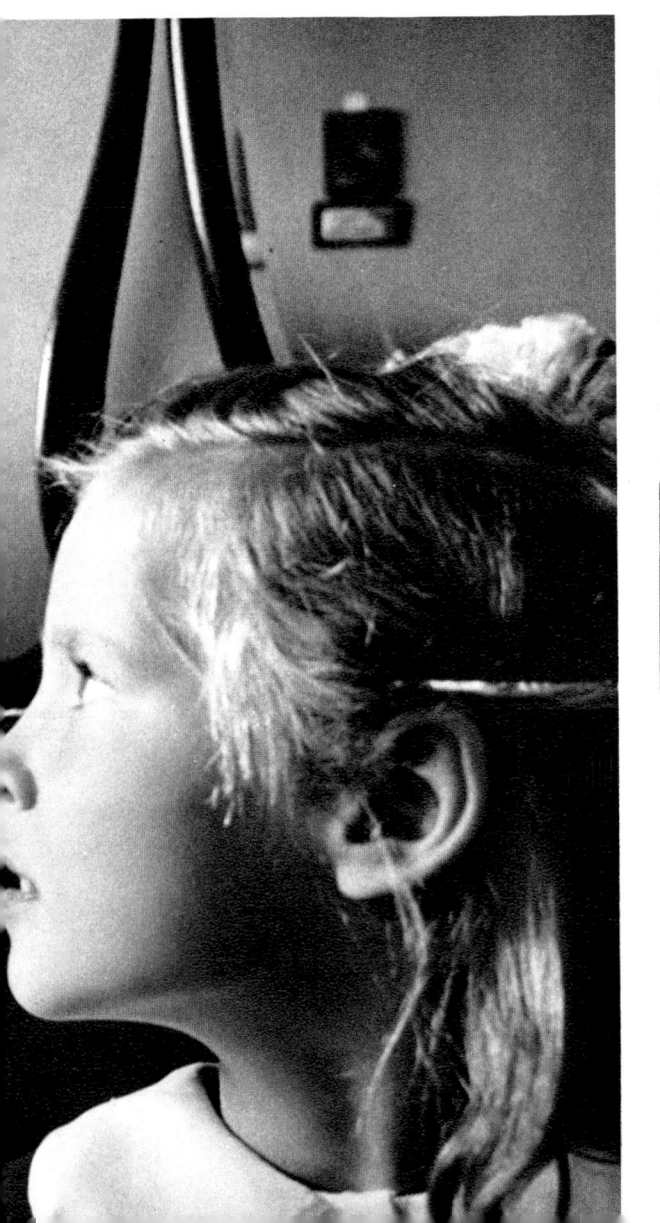

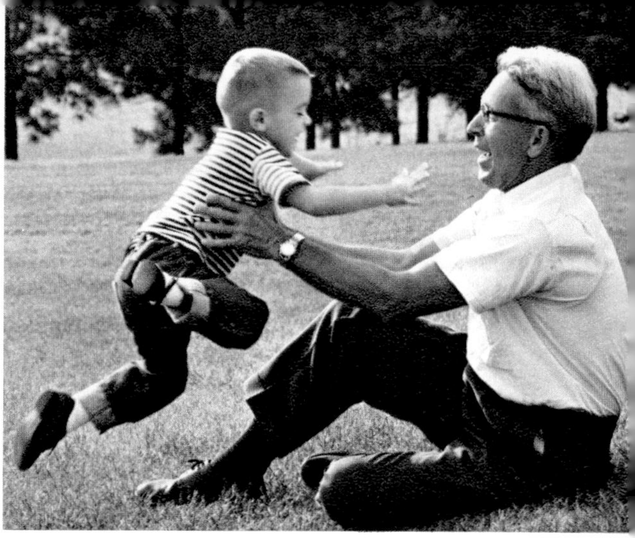

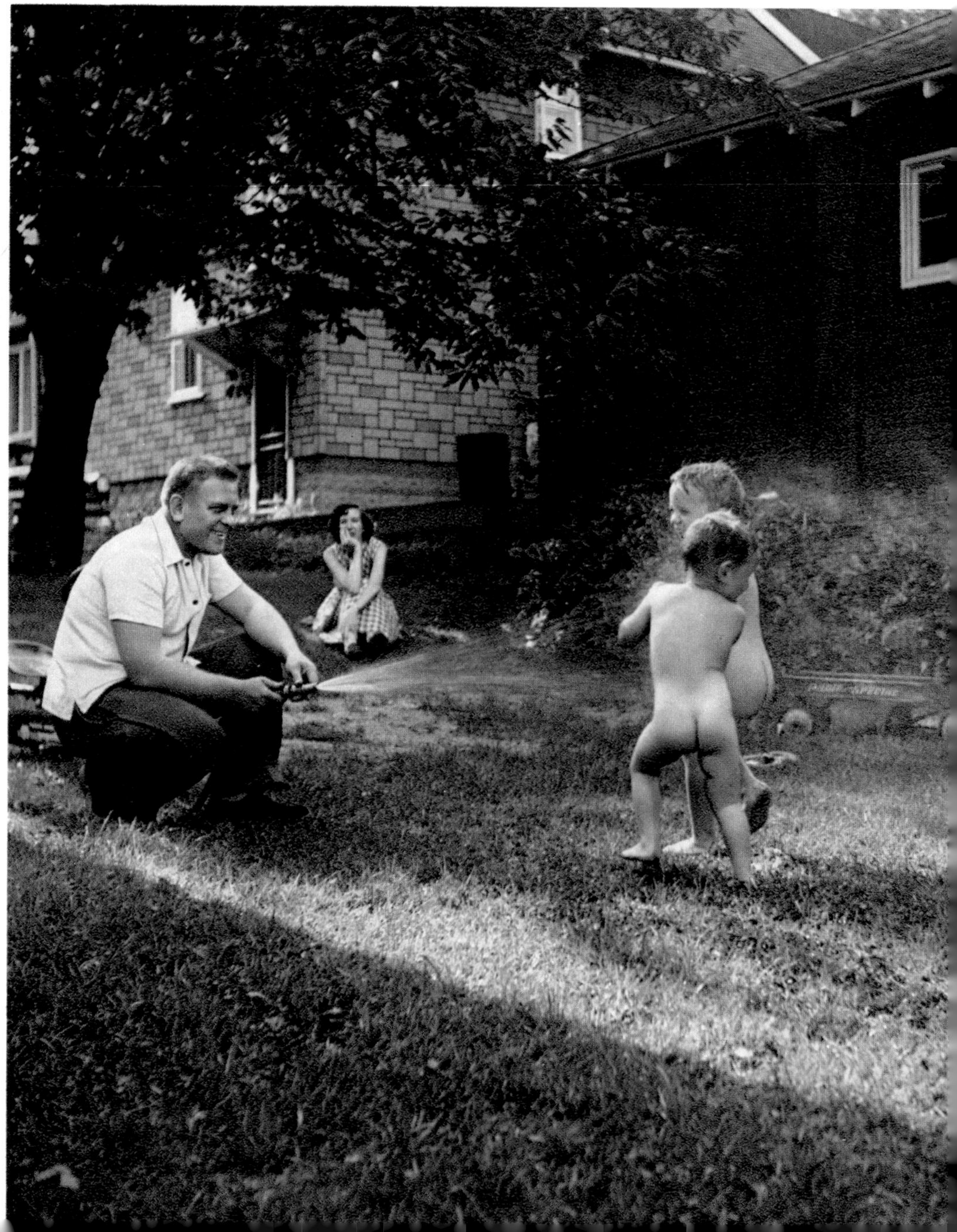

So much of what is great has sprung
from the closeness of family ties.

James Matthew Barrie

Children are principally the creatures of example—whatever surrounding adults do, they will do. If we strike them, they will strike each other.... If we habitually admit the right of sovereignty in each other and in them they will become equally respectful of our rights and of each other's.

Josiah Warren

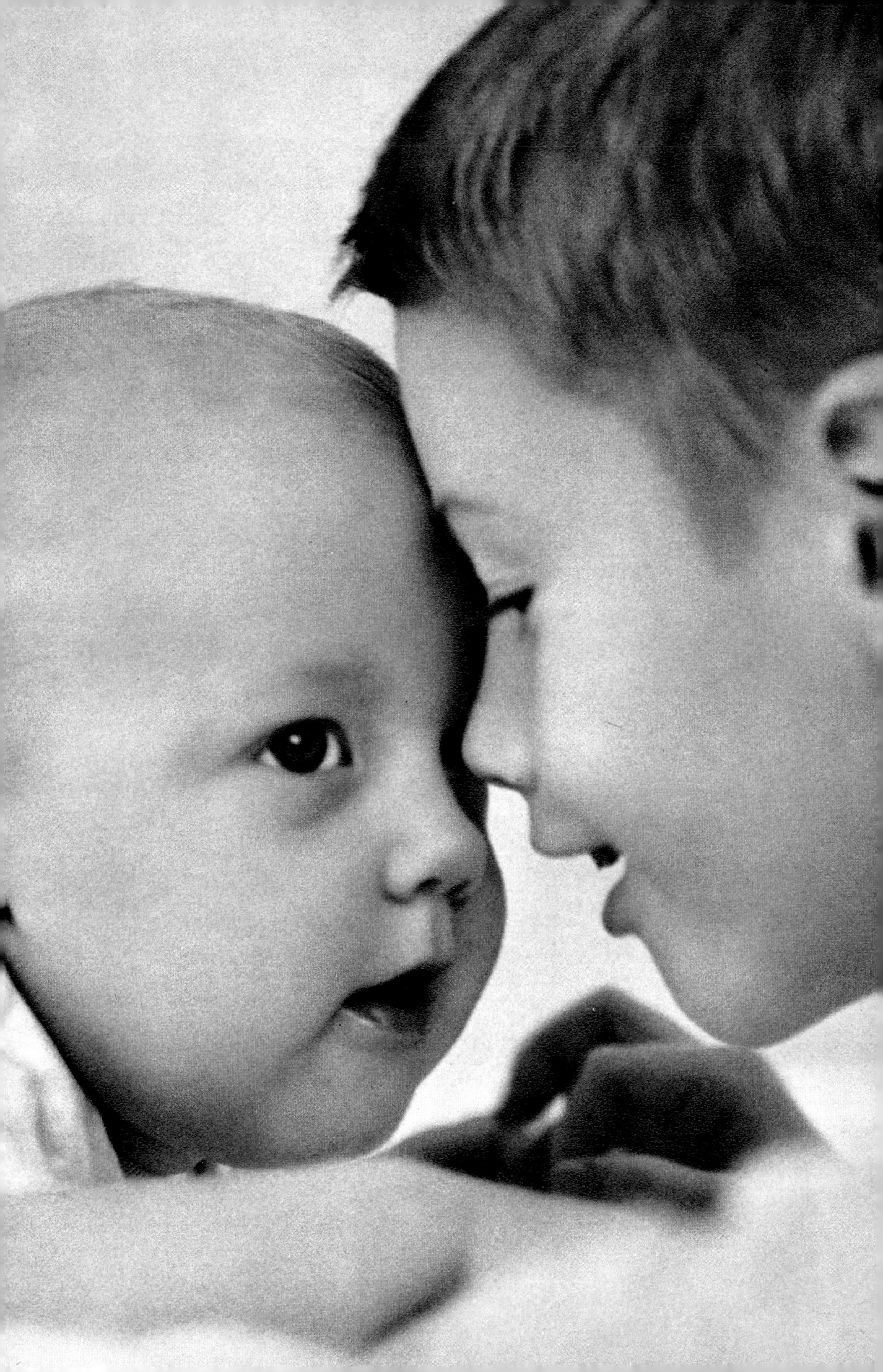

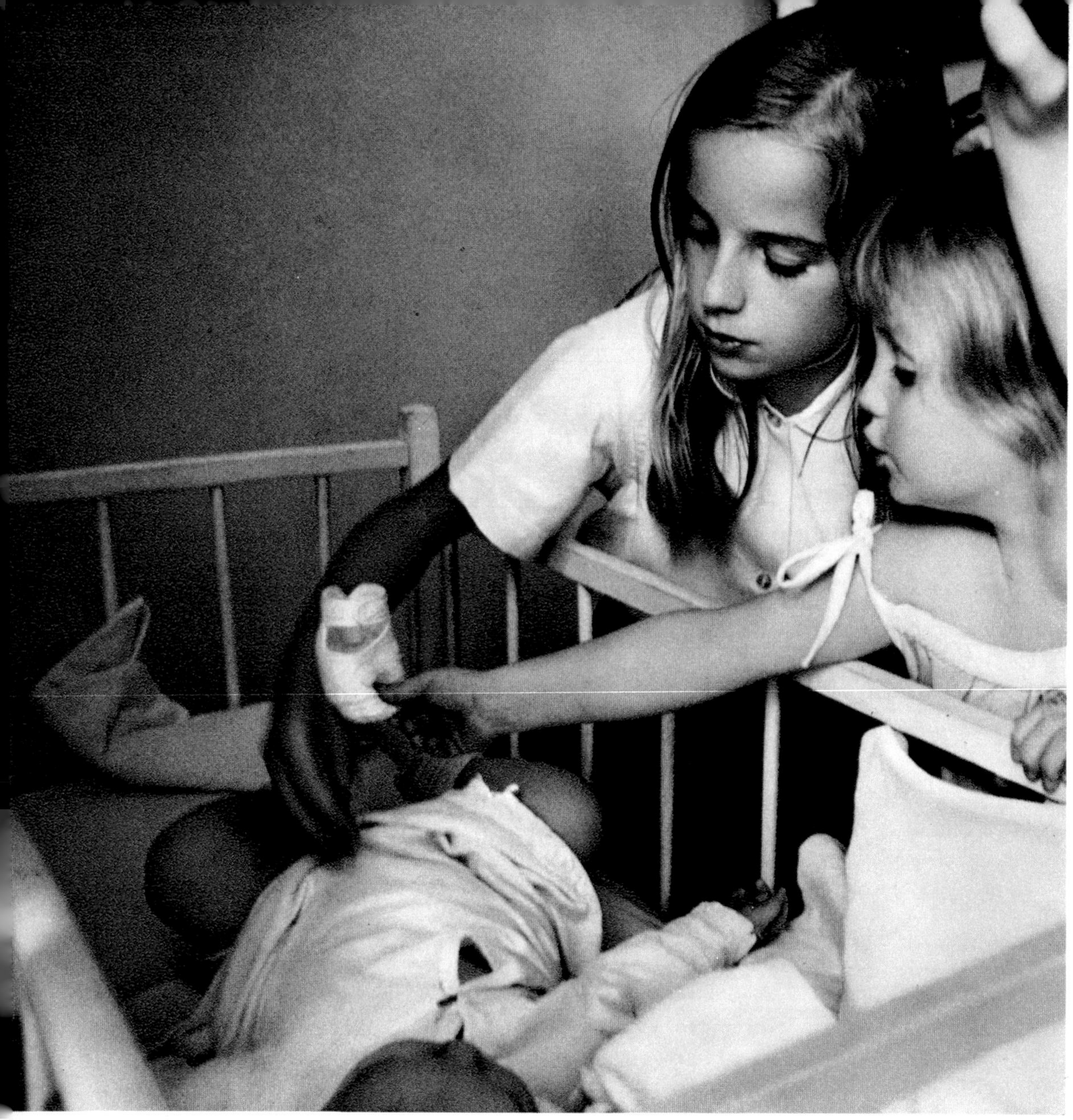

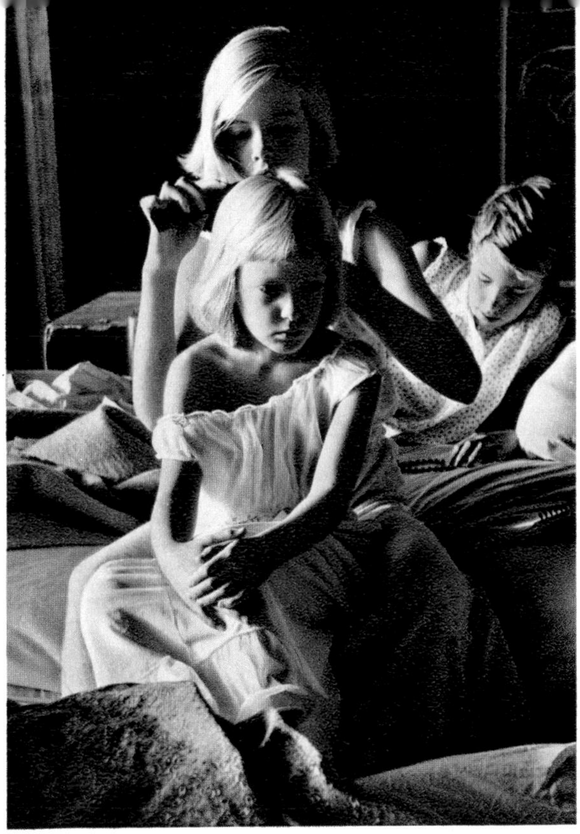

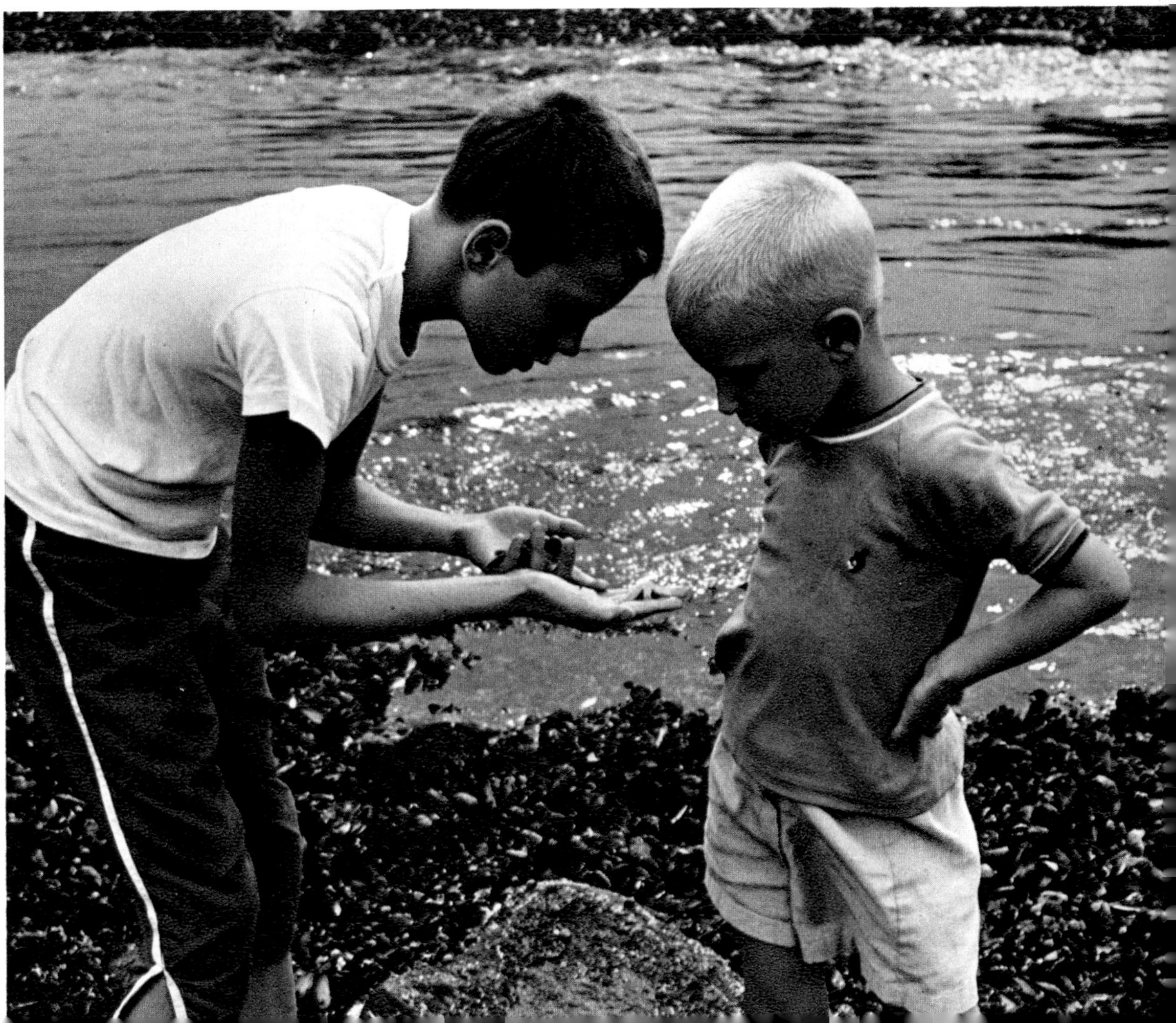

When I am the President
    Of these United States,
I'll eat up all the candy
    And swing on all the gates.

Anonymous

41

Why do the bells of Christmas ring?
   Why do little children sing?
Once a lovely shining star,
     Seen by shepherds from afar,
     Gently moved until its light
     Made a manger's cradle bright.

Eugene Field

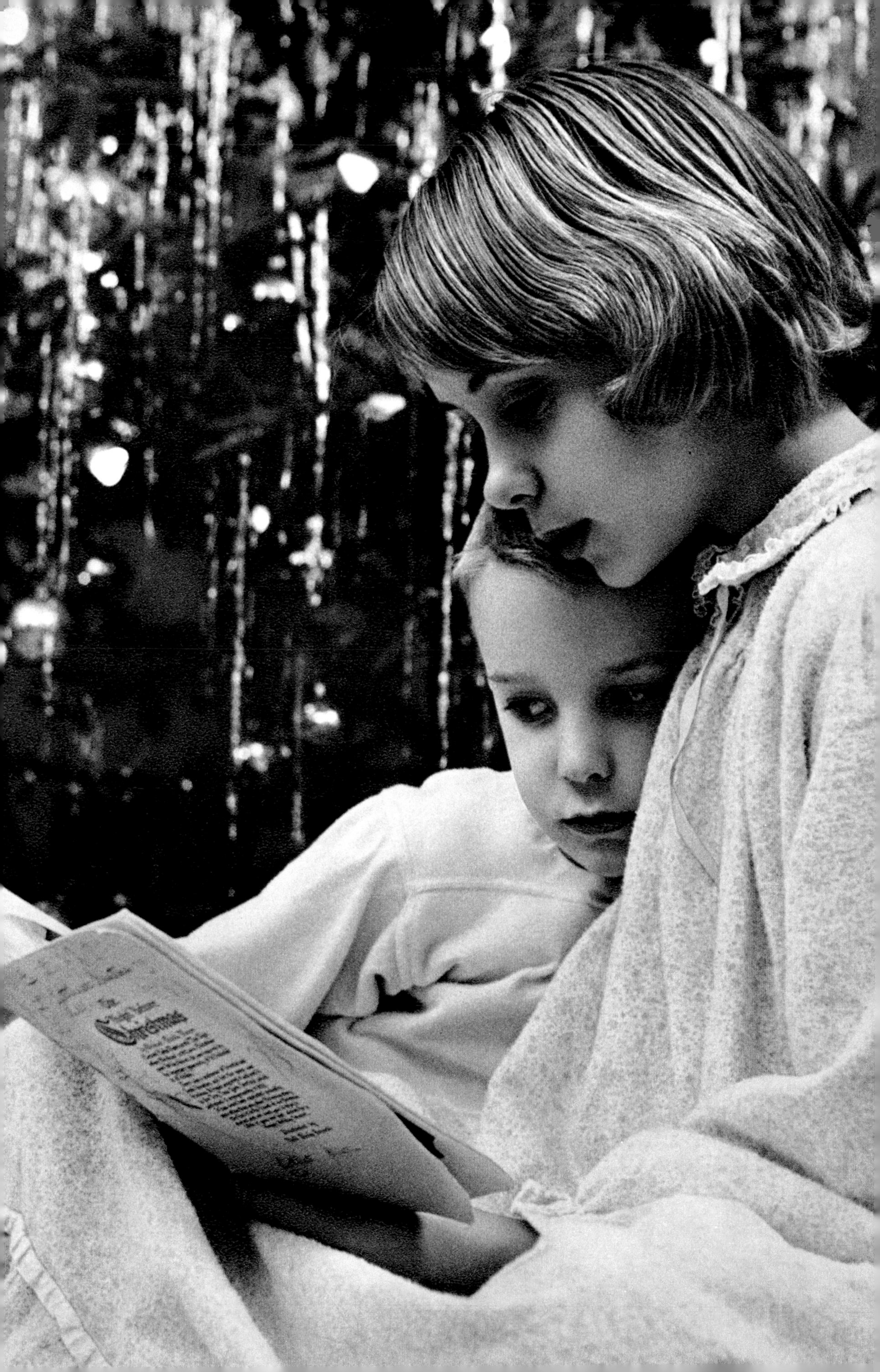

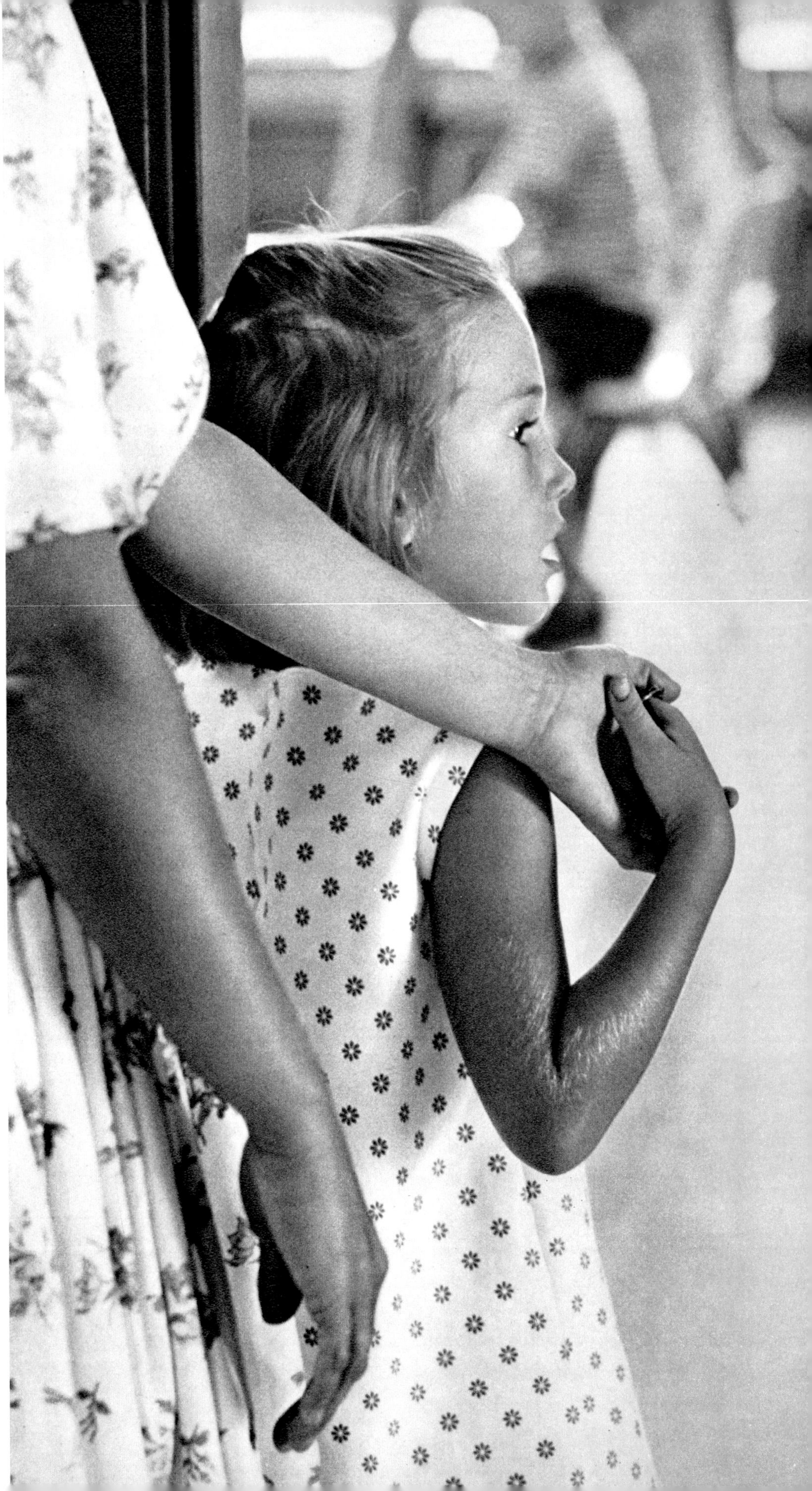

A child's education
should begin at least
a hundred years
before he is born.

Oliver Wendell Holmes

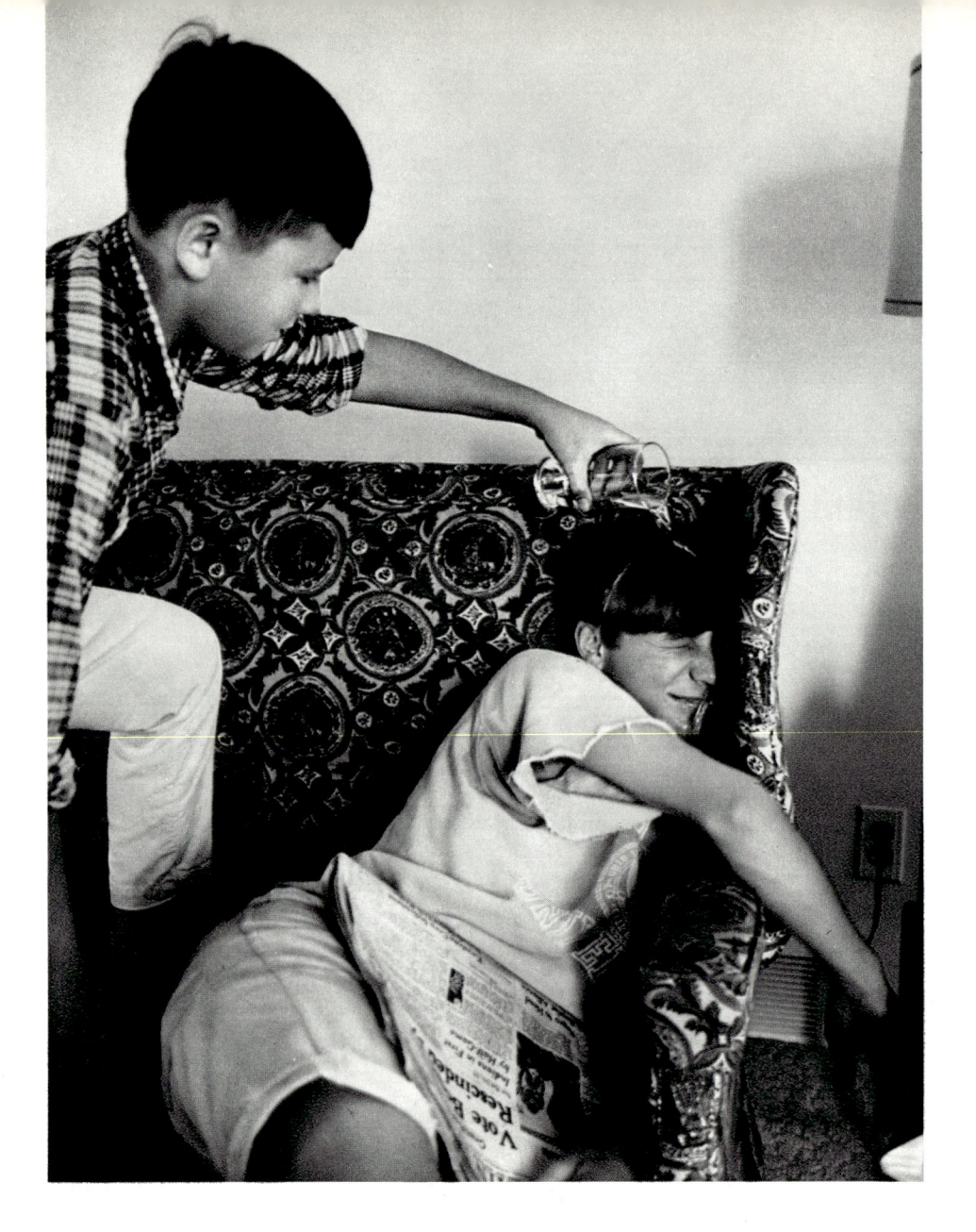

Youth is the time to go flashing from one end of the
world to the other both in mind and body; to try the manners of
different nations; to hear the chimes at midnight;
to see sunrise in town and country; to be converted at a revival;
to circumnavigate the metaphysics, write halting verses,
run a mile to see a fire.

Robert Louis Stevenson

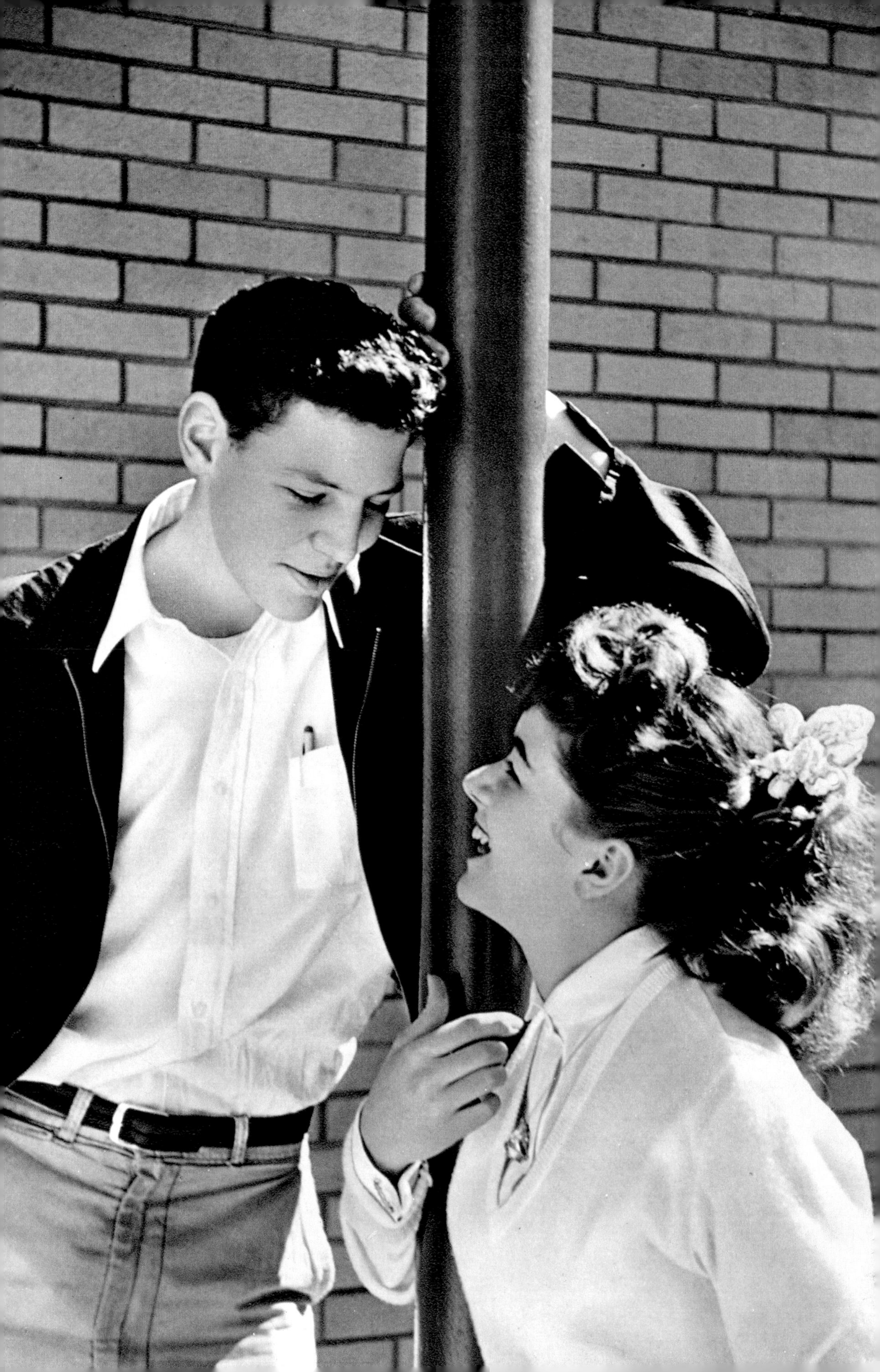

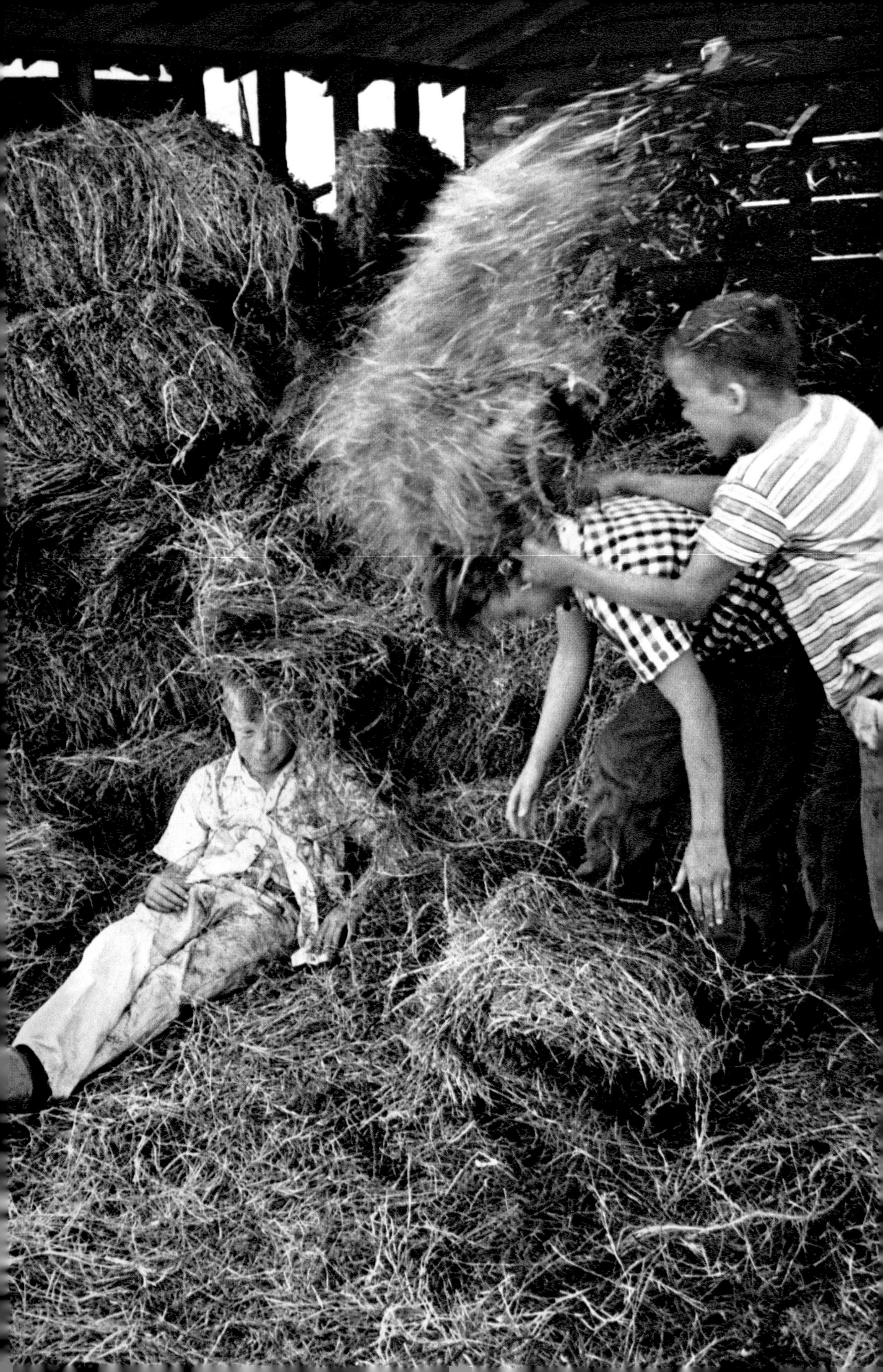

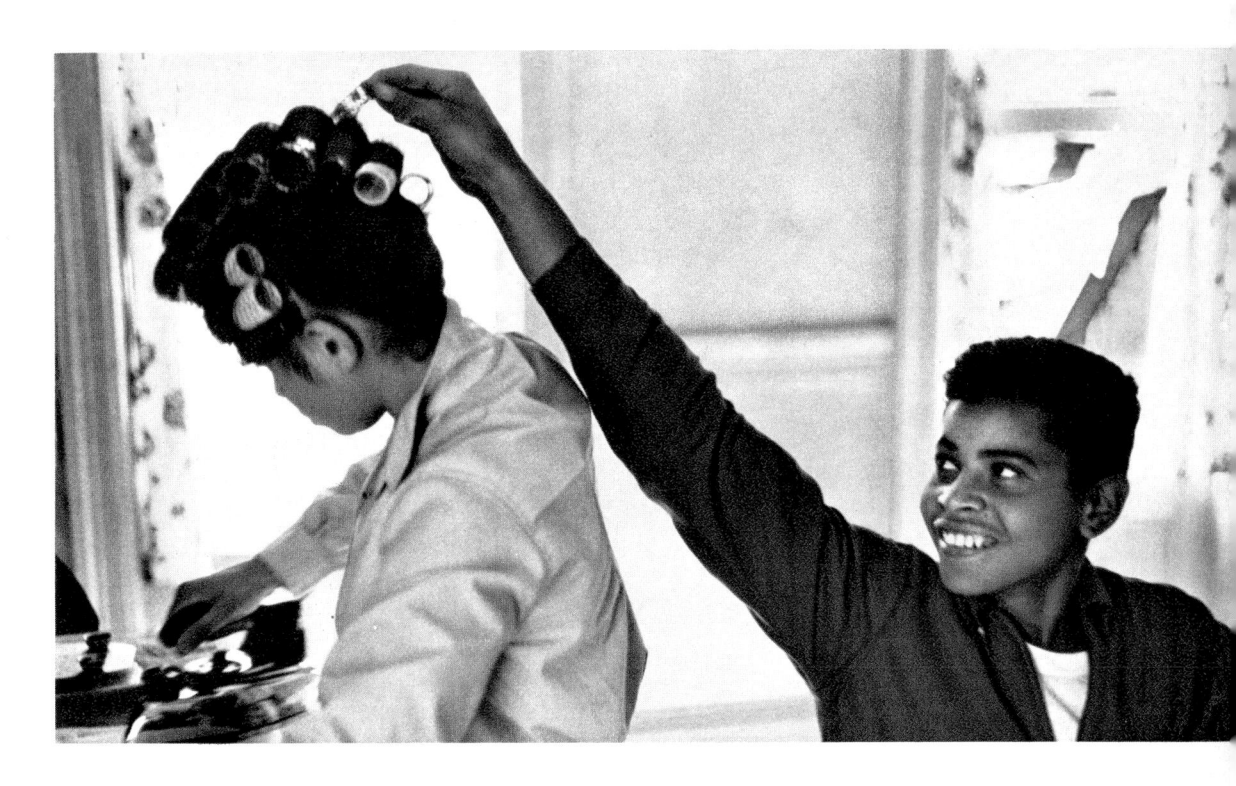

Youth, large, lusty, loving—youth full of grace, force, fascination, do you know that Old Age may come after you with equal grace, force, fascination?

Walt Whitman

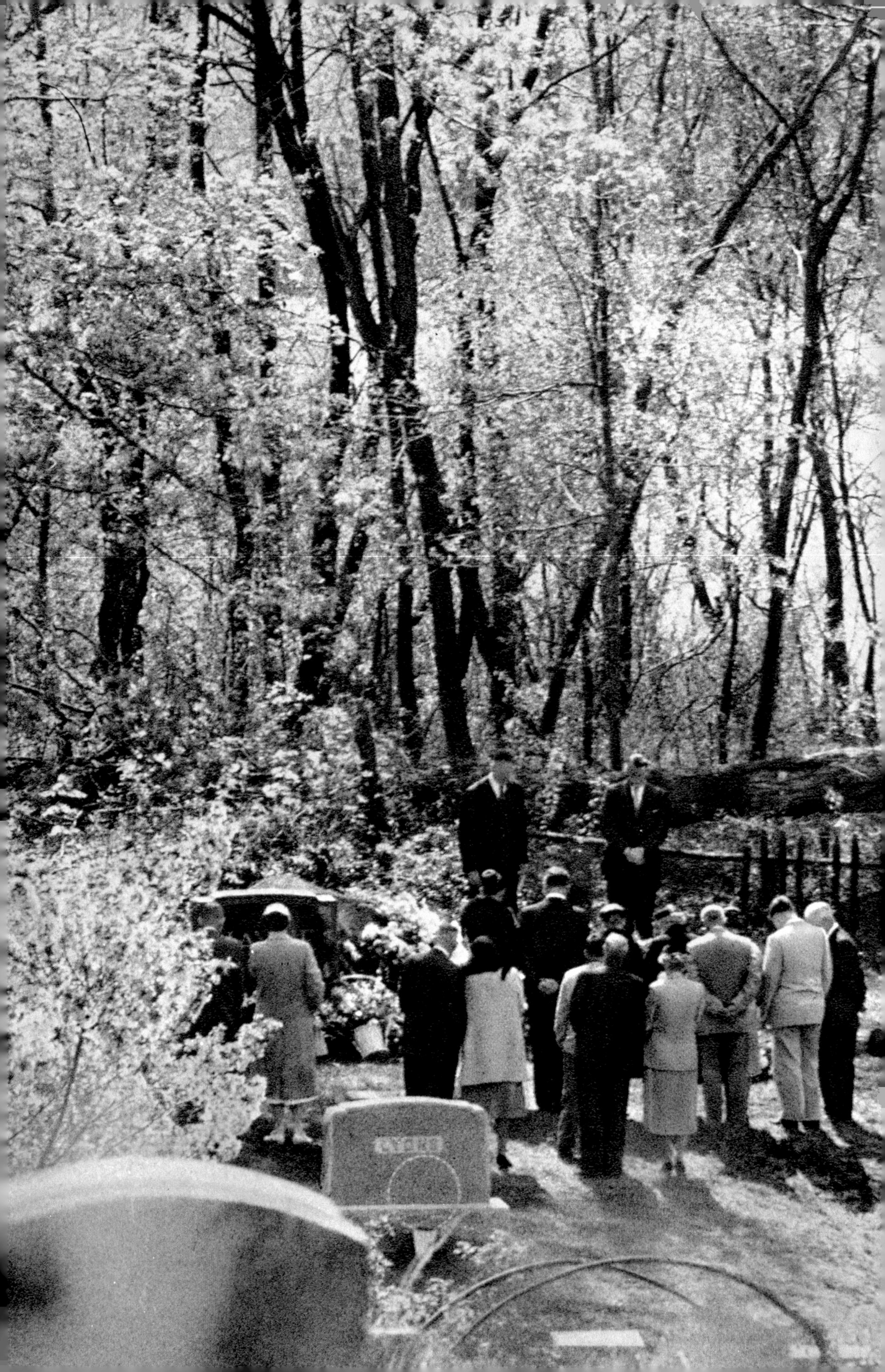

We understand death for the first time when he puts his hand upon one whom we love.

Madame de Staël

As a white candle
In a holy place,
So is the beauty
Of an aged face.

Joseph Campbell

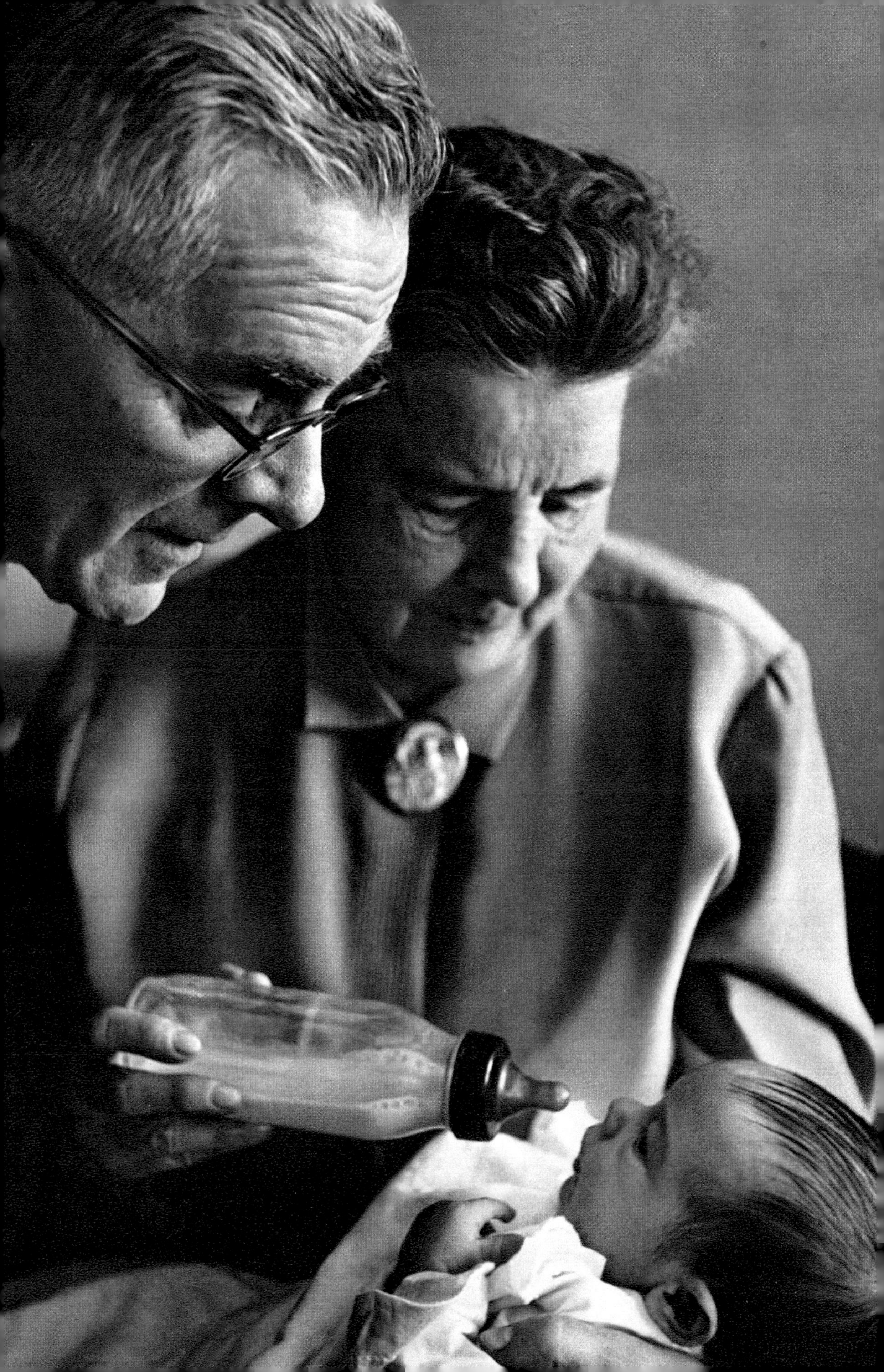

To make your children capable of honesty is the beginning of education.

John Ruskin

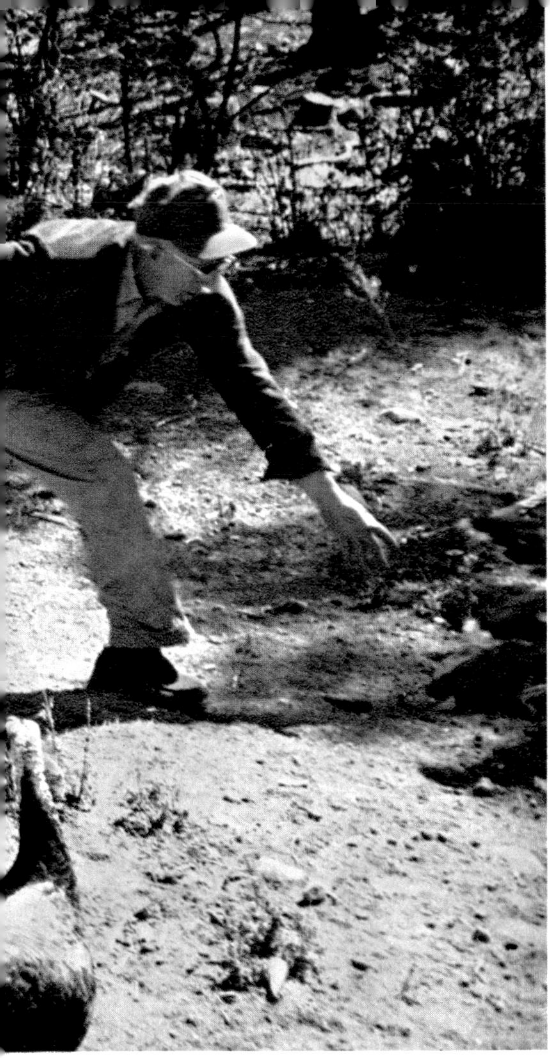

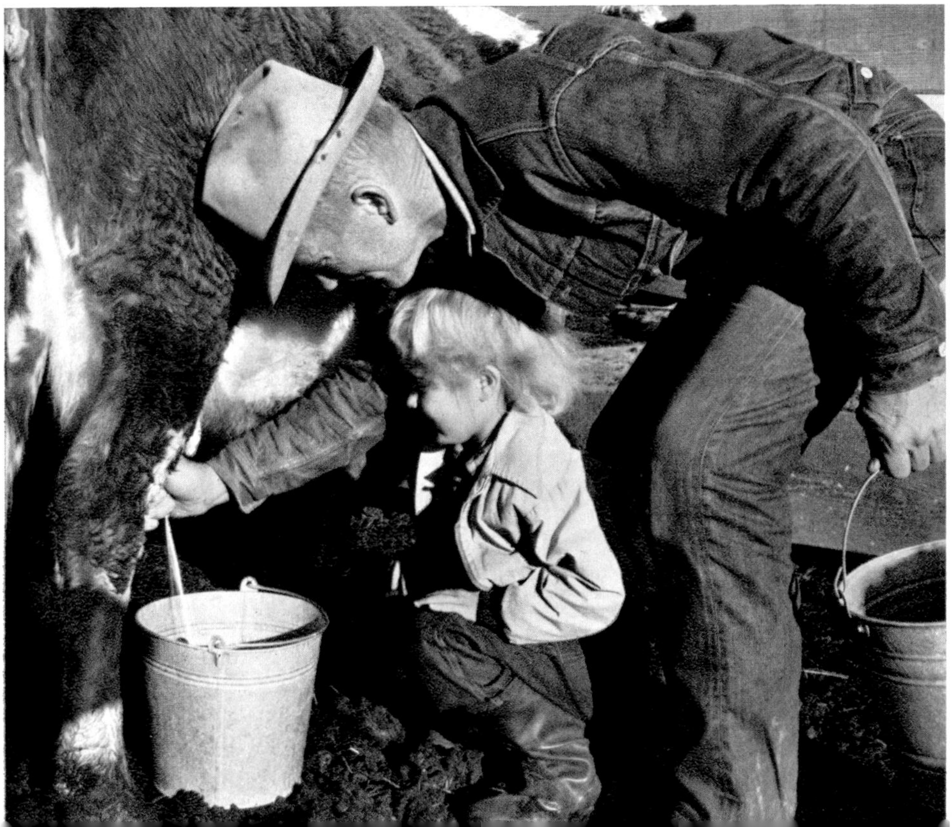

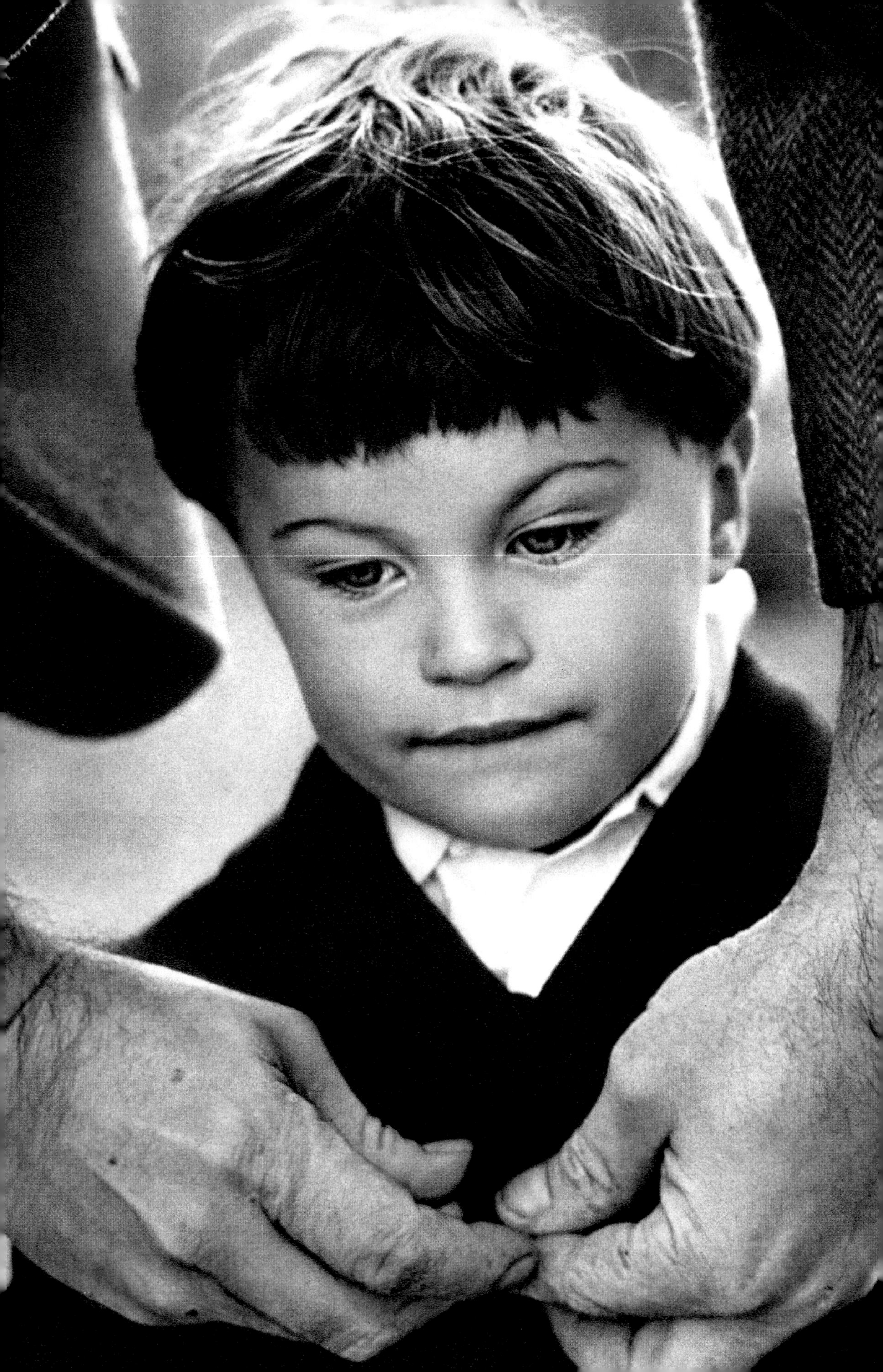

My heart is at rest within my breast,
And everything else is still.

William Blake

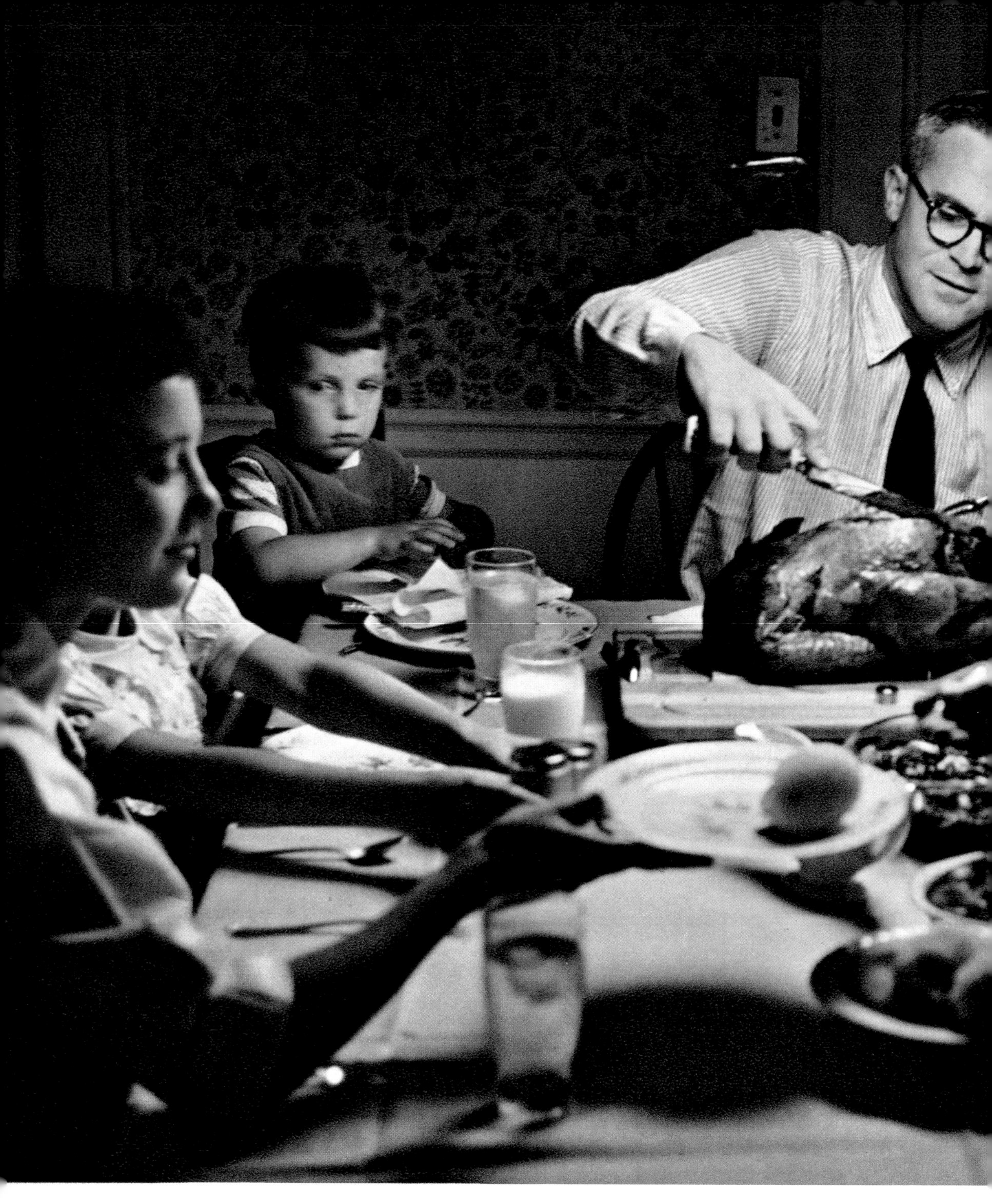

Good family life is never an accident
but always an achievement by those who share it.

James H.S. Bossard

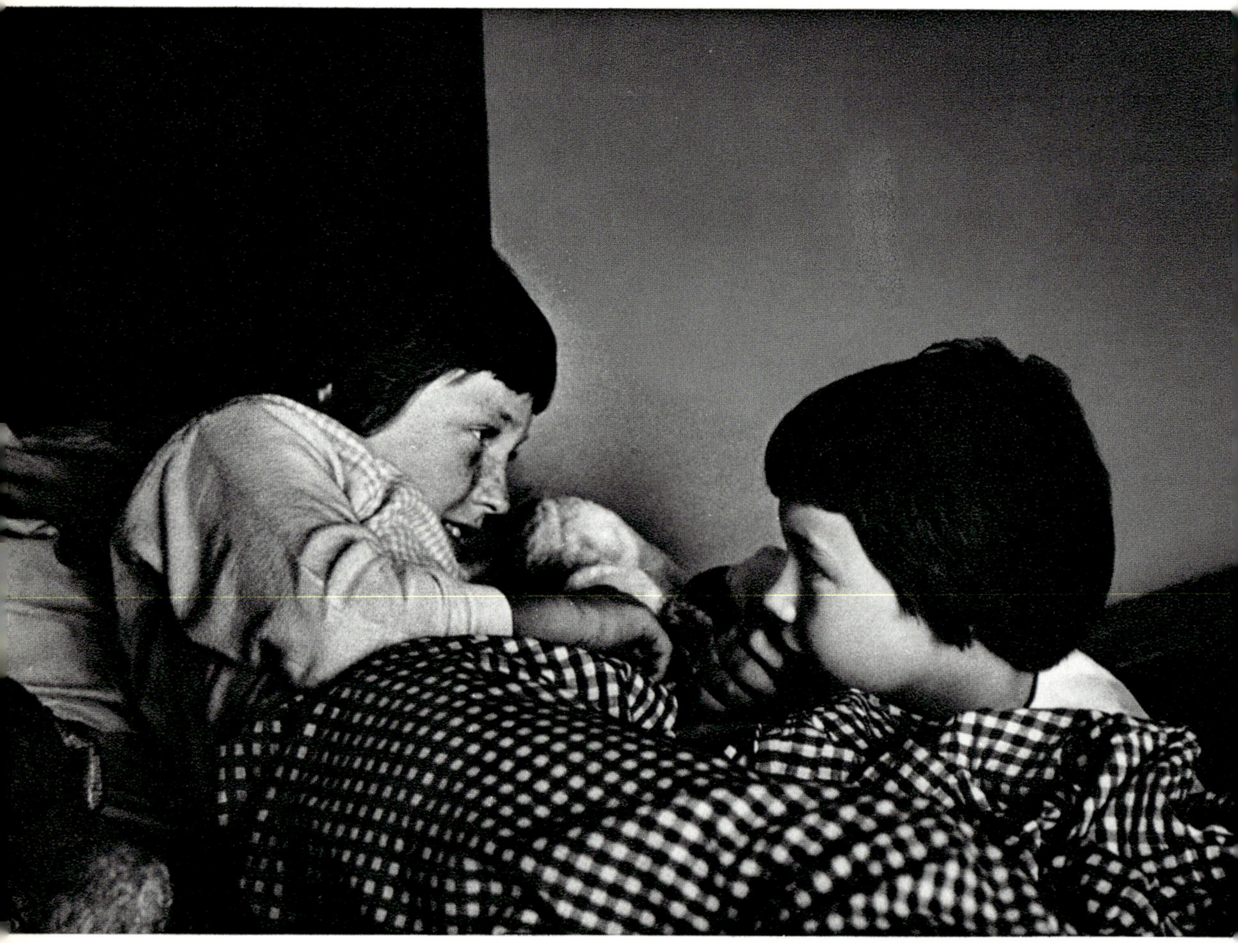

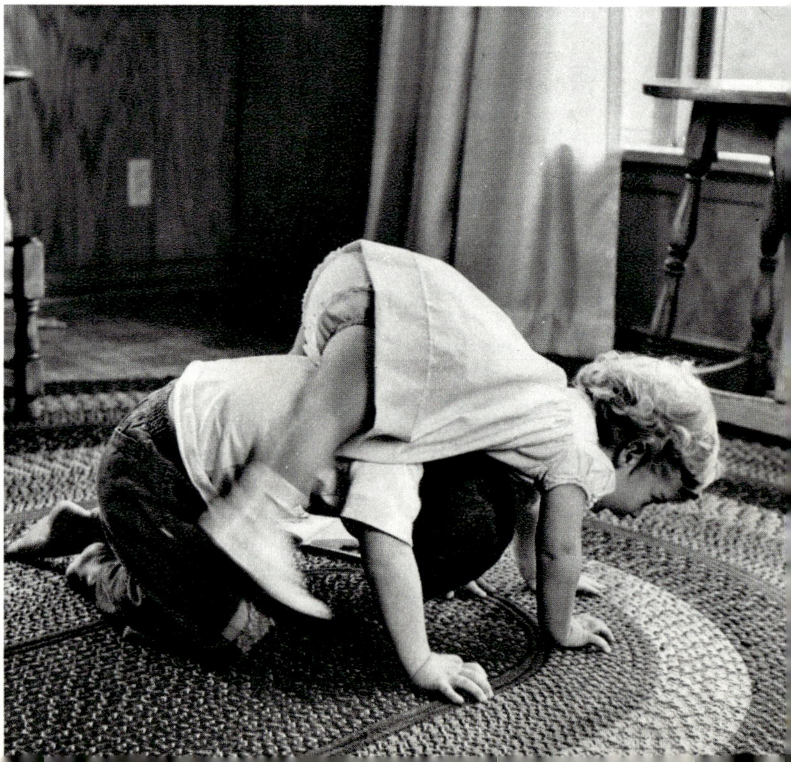

Be like the bird
That, pausing in her flight
Awhile on boughs too slight
   Feels them give way
Beneath her and yet sings,
Knowing that she hath wings.

Victor Hugo

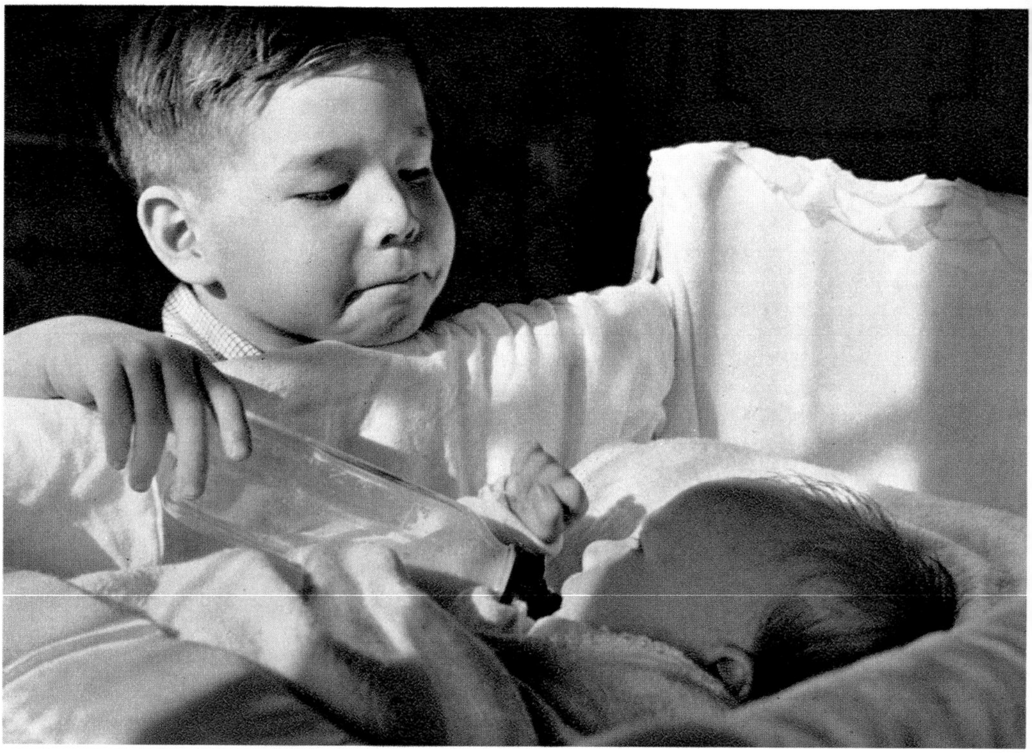

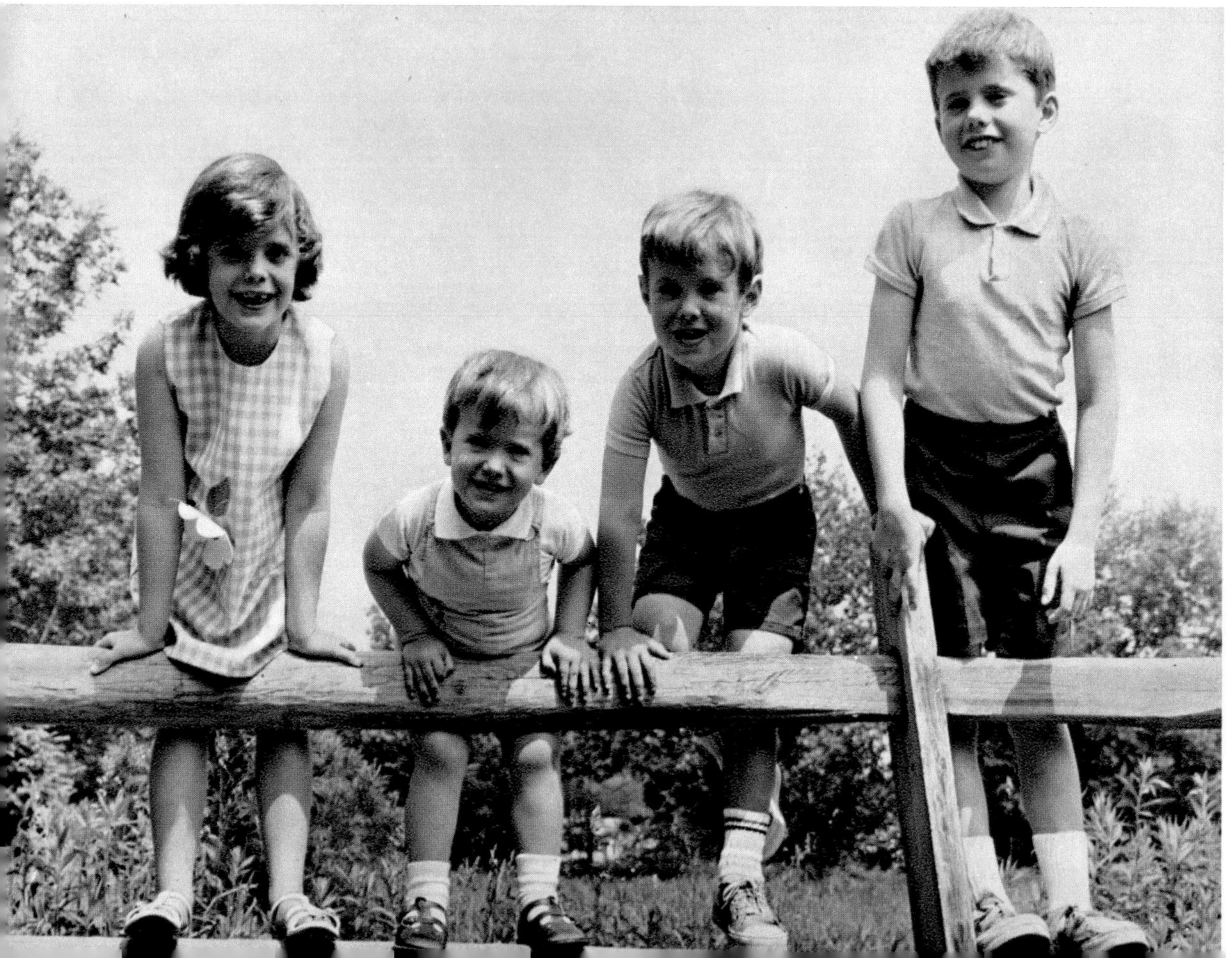

Sweet childish days, that were as long as twenty days are now.

William Wordsworth

There is an enduring tenderness in the love of a mother to a son that transcends all other affections of the heart... she will glory in his fame and exult in his prosperity; and, if adversity overtake him, he will be the dearer to her by misfortune.

Washington Irving

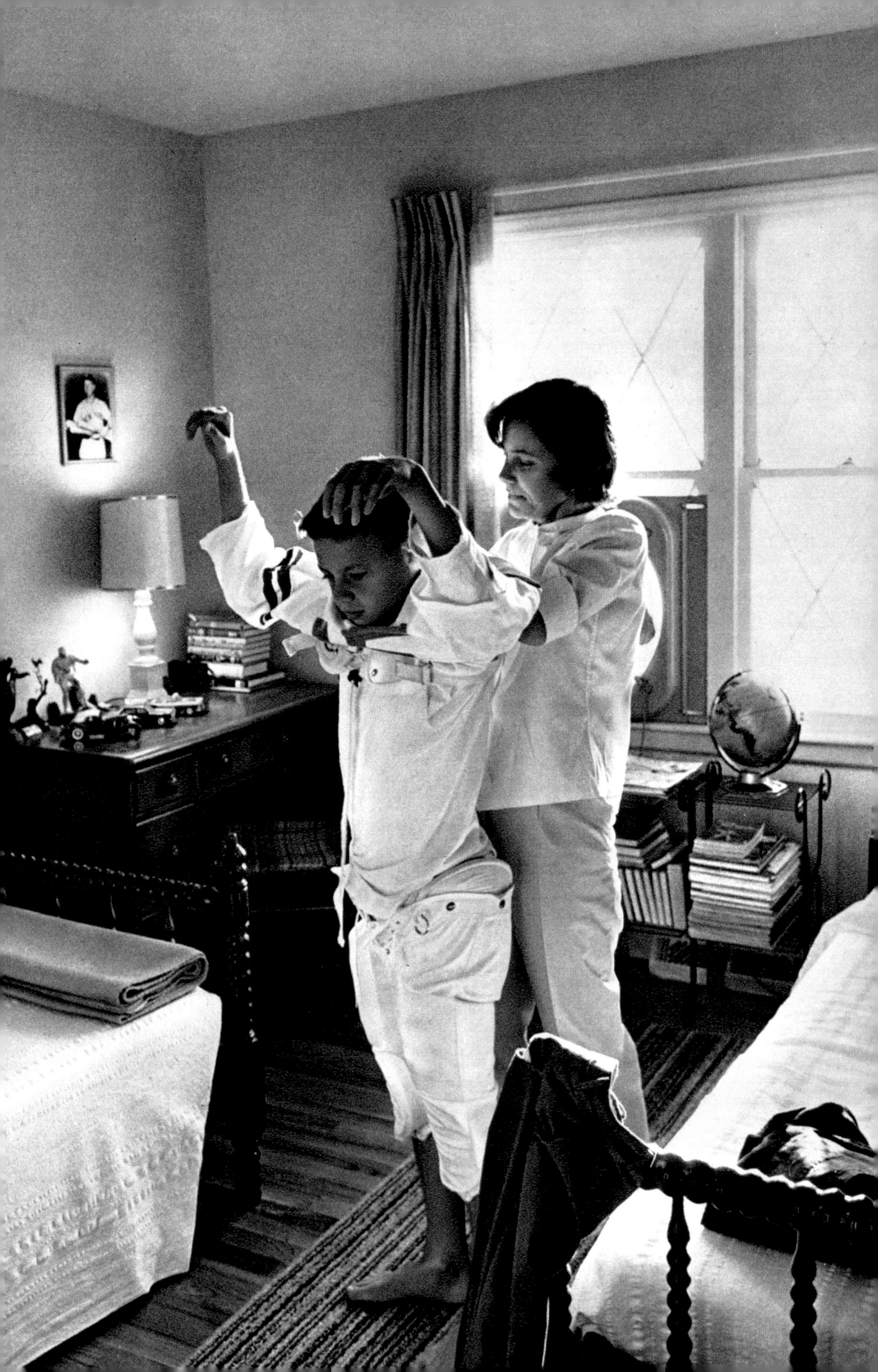

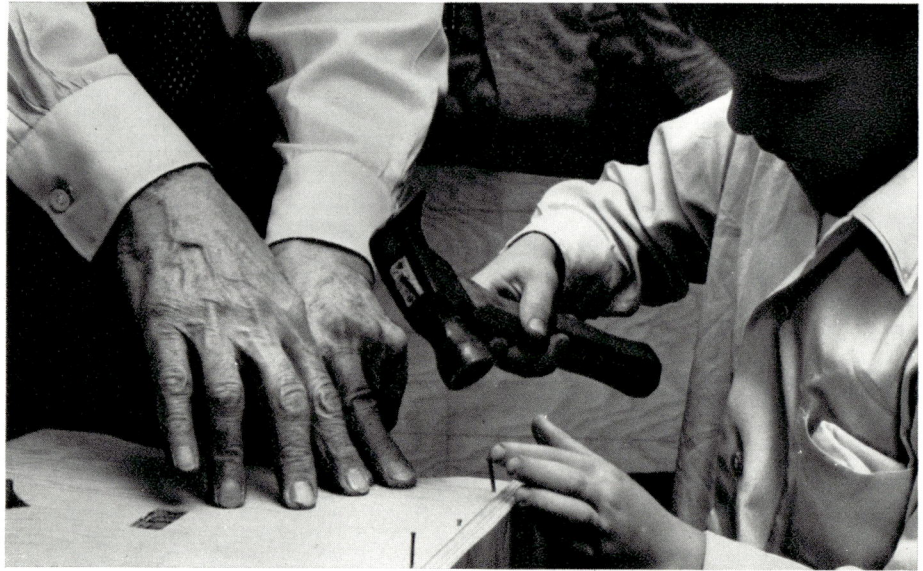

I was ever of the opinion, that the honest man who married and brought up a large family, did more service than he who continued single and only talked of population.

Oliver Goldsmith

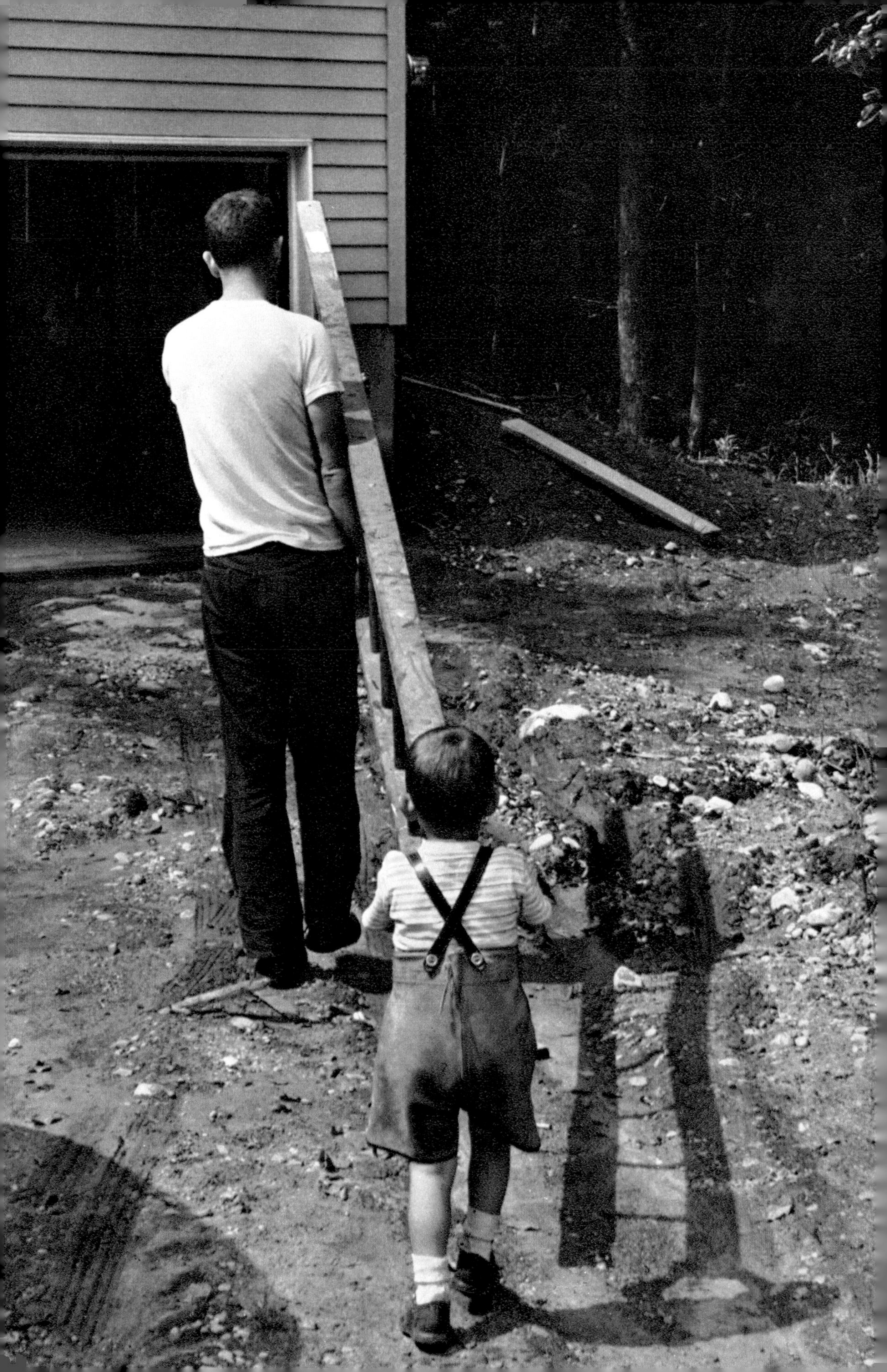

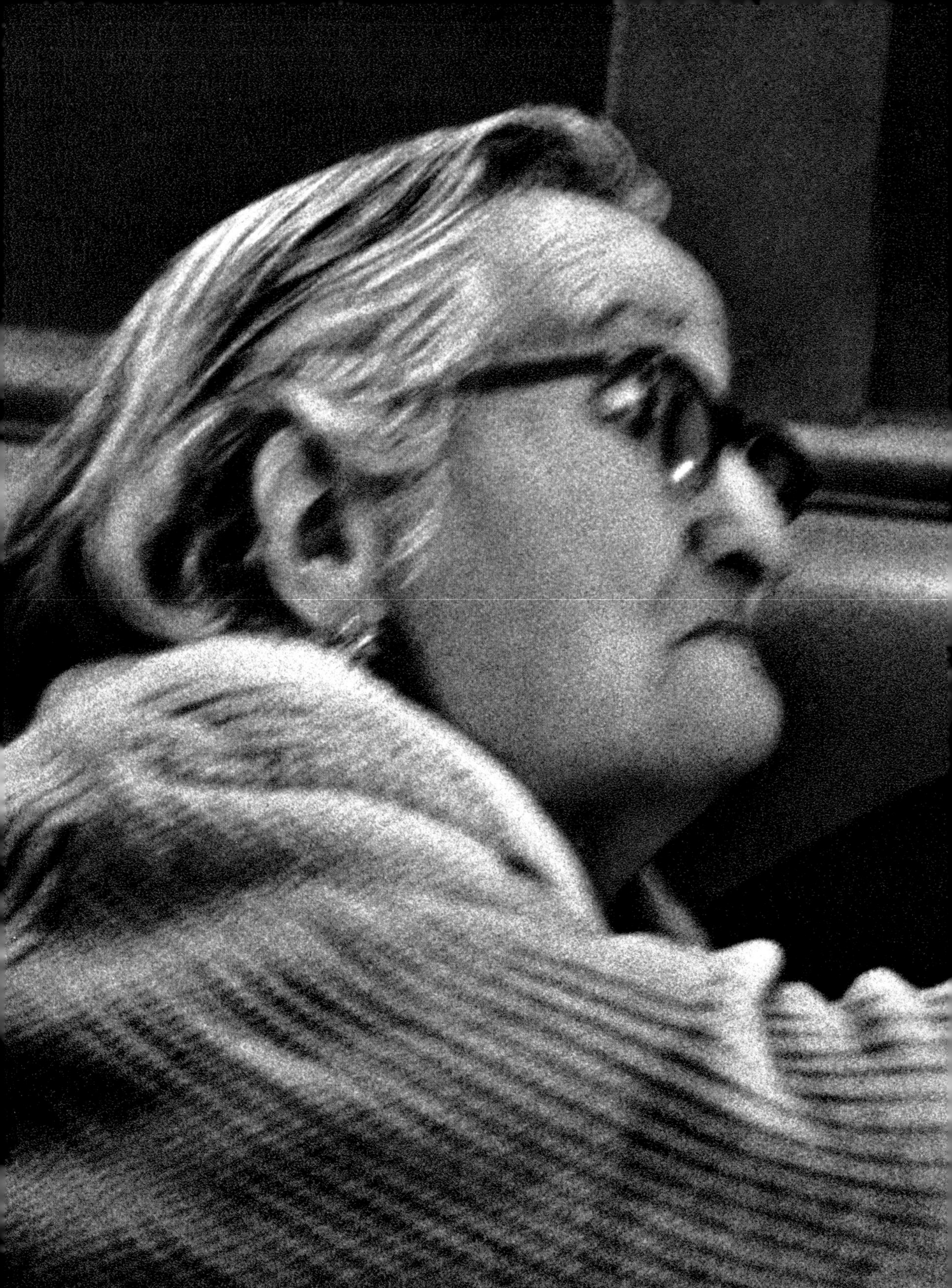

There is a peculiar beauty
about godly old age—the
beauty of holiness.
Husband and wife who have
fought the world side by
side, who have made common
stock of joy or sorrow,
and become aged together,
are not unfrequently found
curiously alike in personal
appearance, in pitch and
tone of voice, just as
twin pebbles on the beach,
exposed to the same tidal
influences, are each
other's alter ego.

Alexander Smith

What is the little one thinking about?
Very wonderful things, no doubt;
Unwritten history!
Unfathomed mystery!
Yet he laughs, and cries, and eats, and drinks.
And chuckles and crows, and laughs and winks,
As if his head were as full of kinks
And curious riddles as any Sphinx.

Josiah Gilbert Holland

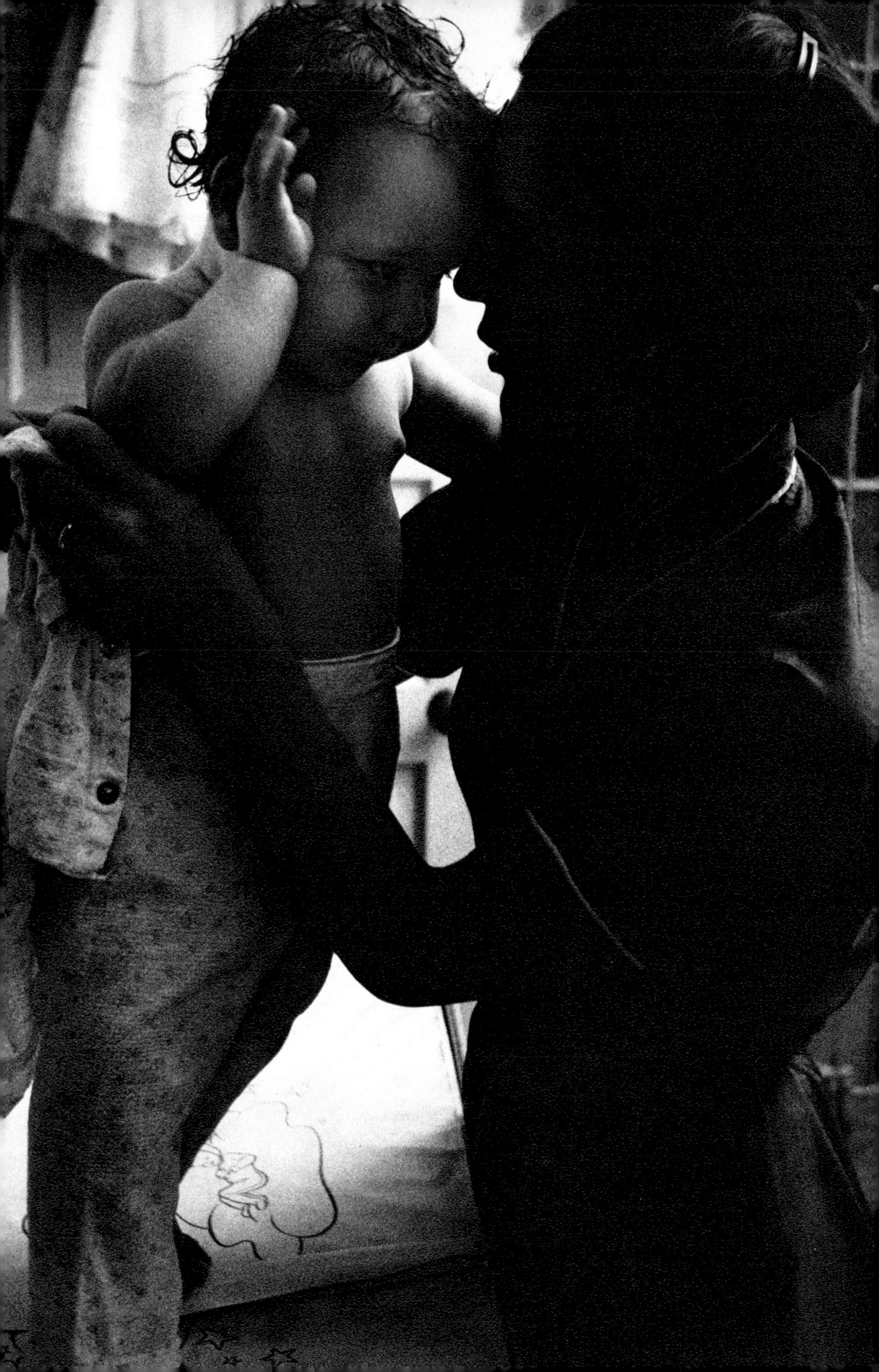

God, what a world, if men in street and mart
Felt that same kinship of the human heart
Which makes them, in the face of fire and flood,
Rise to the meaning of True Brotherhood.

Ella Wheeler Wilcox

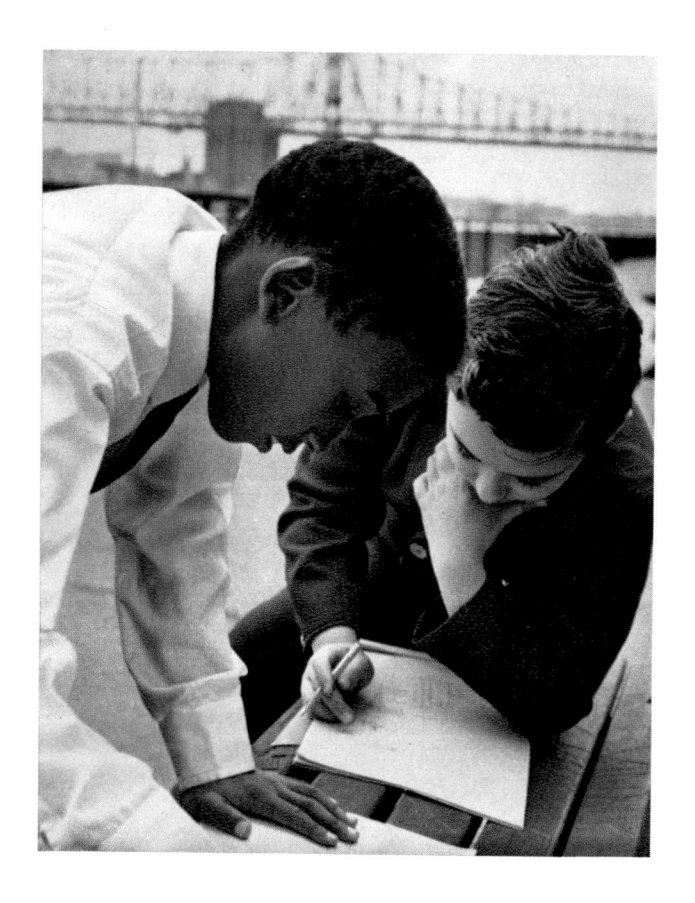

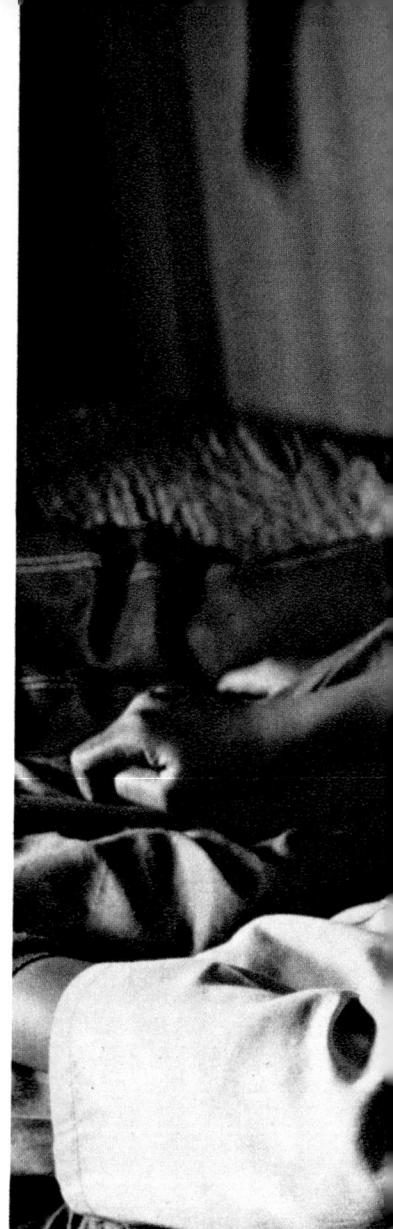

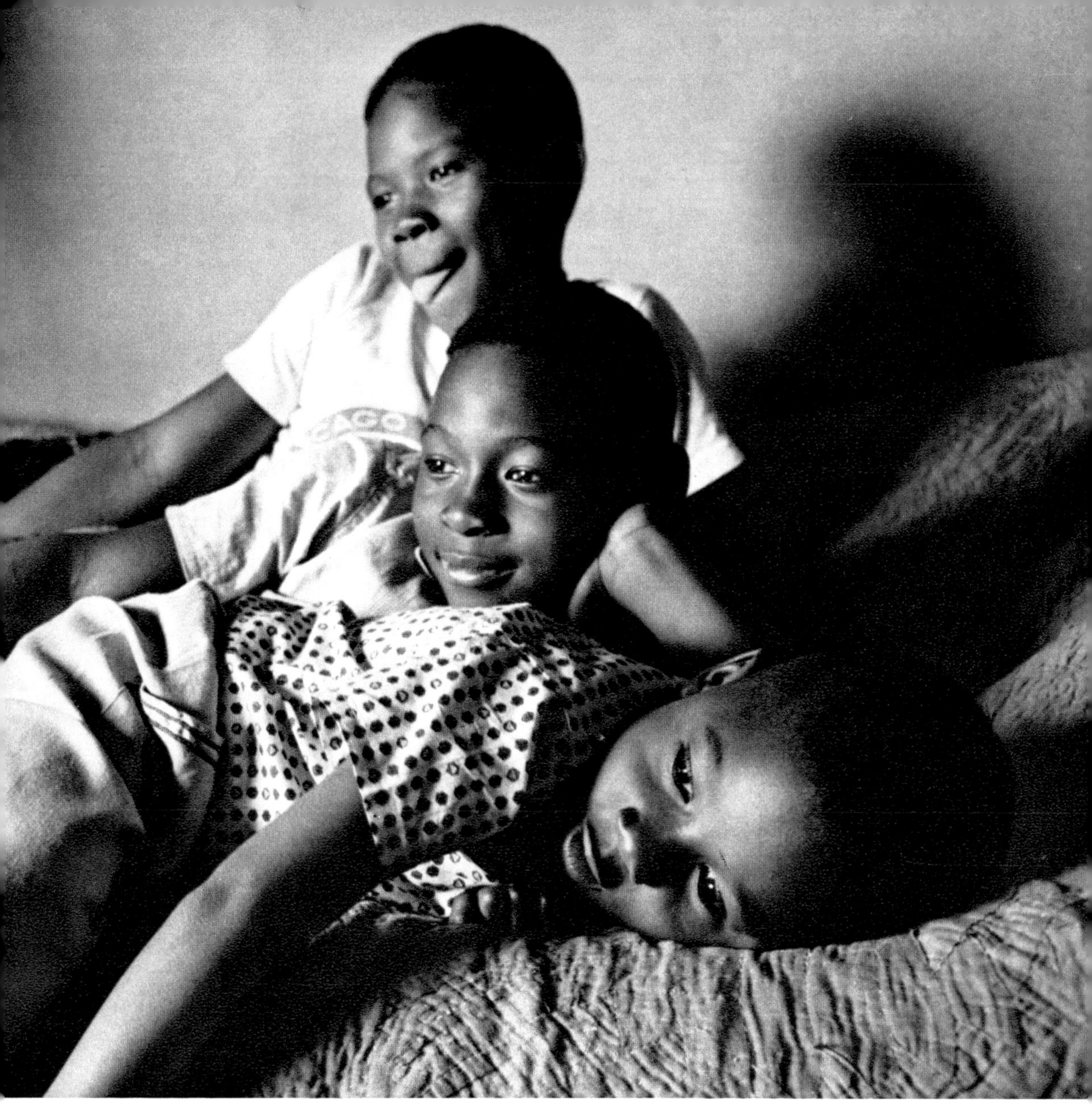

We ought to hear at least one little song every day, read a good poem, see a first-rate painting, and if possible speak a few sensible words.

Johann Wolfgang von Goethe

If a man does not keep pace with his companions, perhaps it is because he hears a different drummer. Let him step to the music he hears, however measured or far away.

Henry David Thoreau

The youth gets together his materials to build a bridge to the moon, or, perchance, a palace or temple on the earth...

Henry David Thoreau

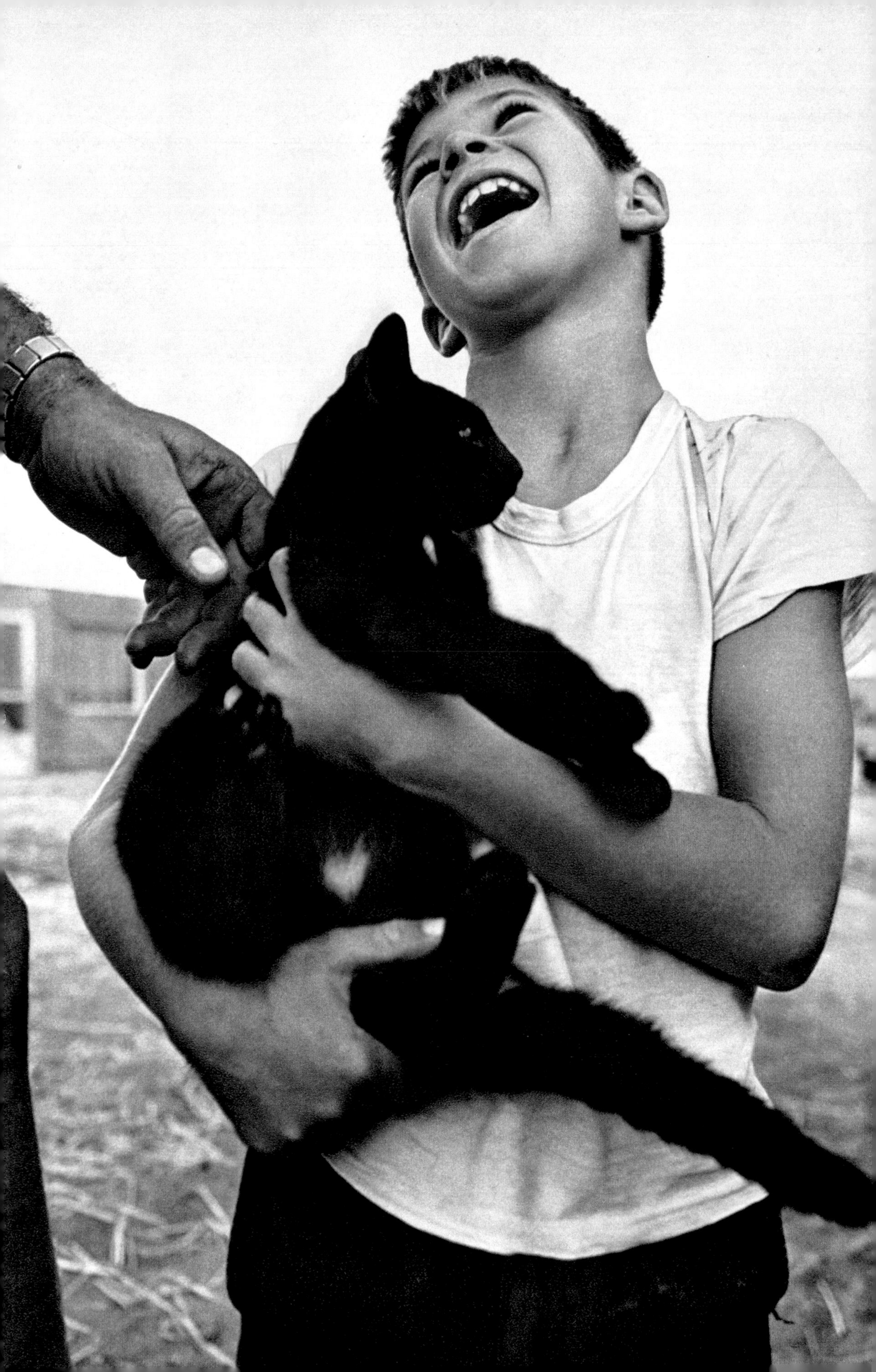

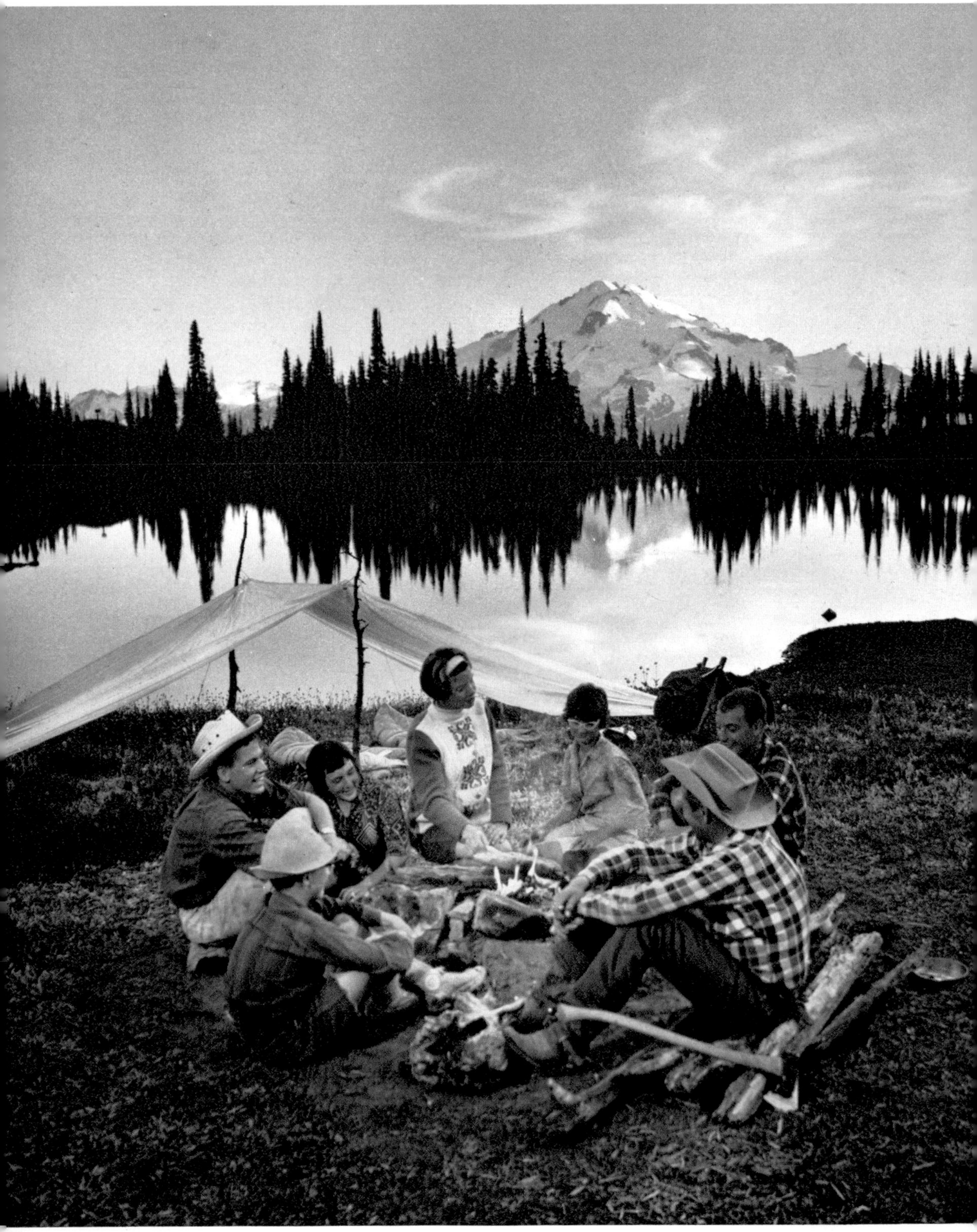

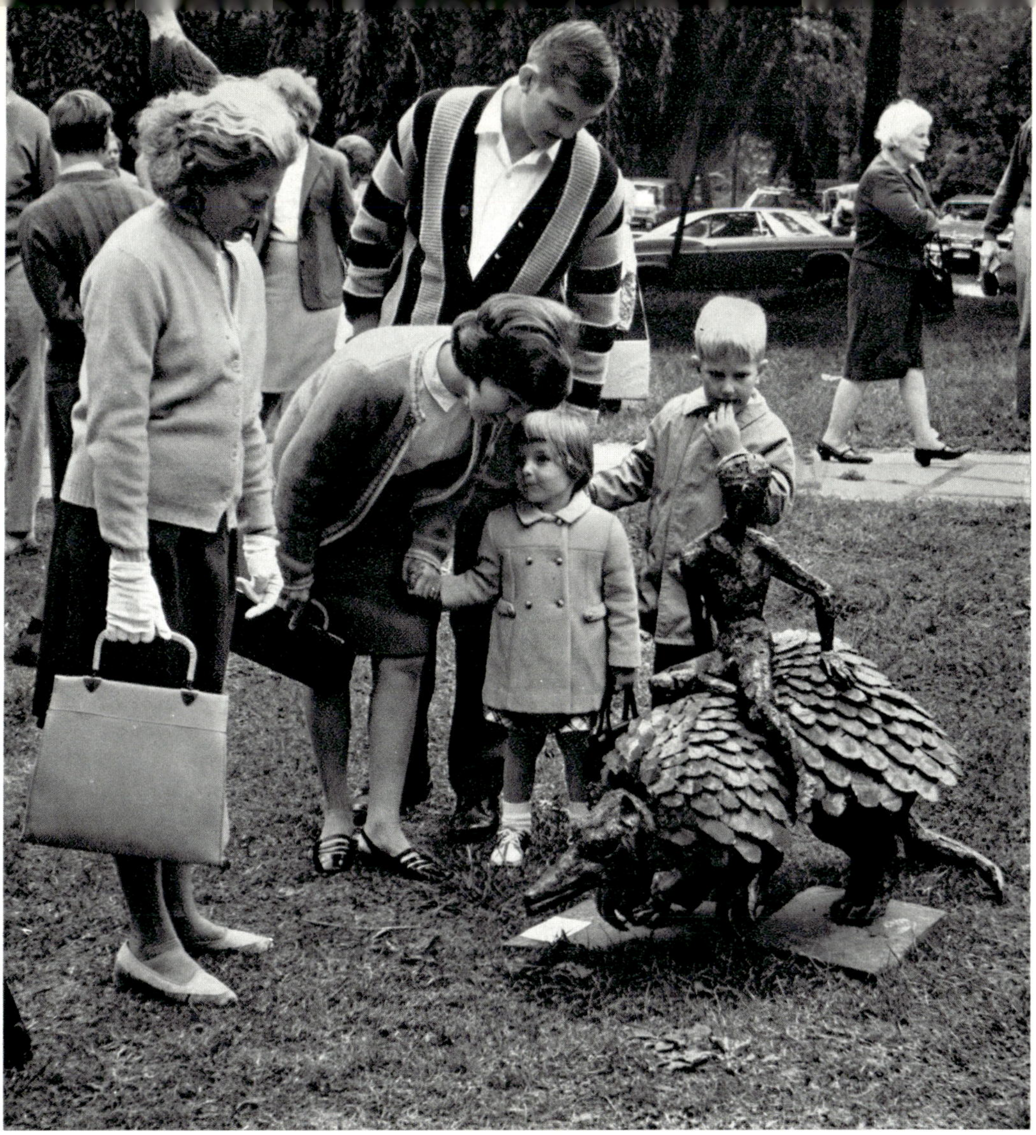

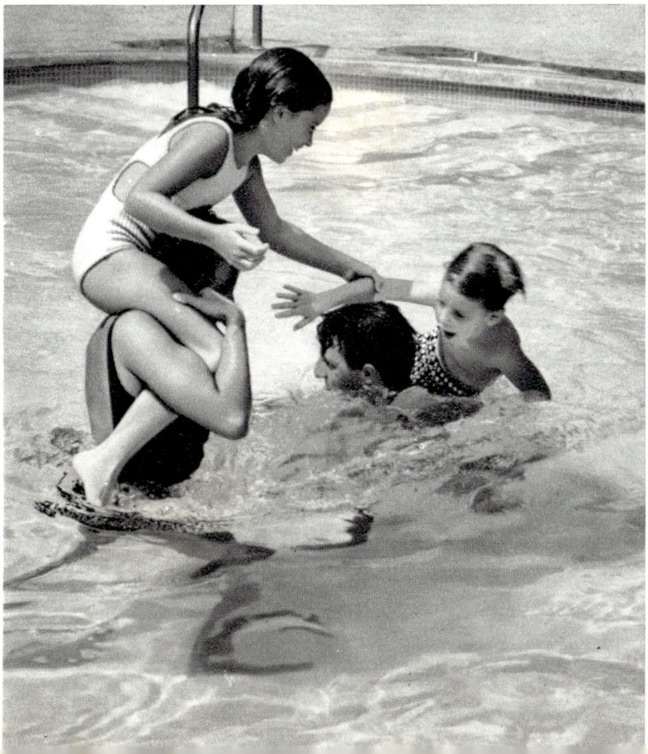

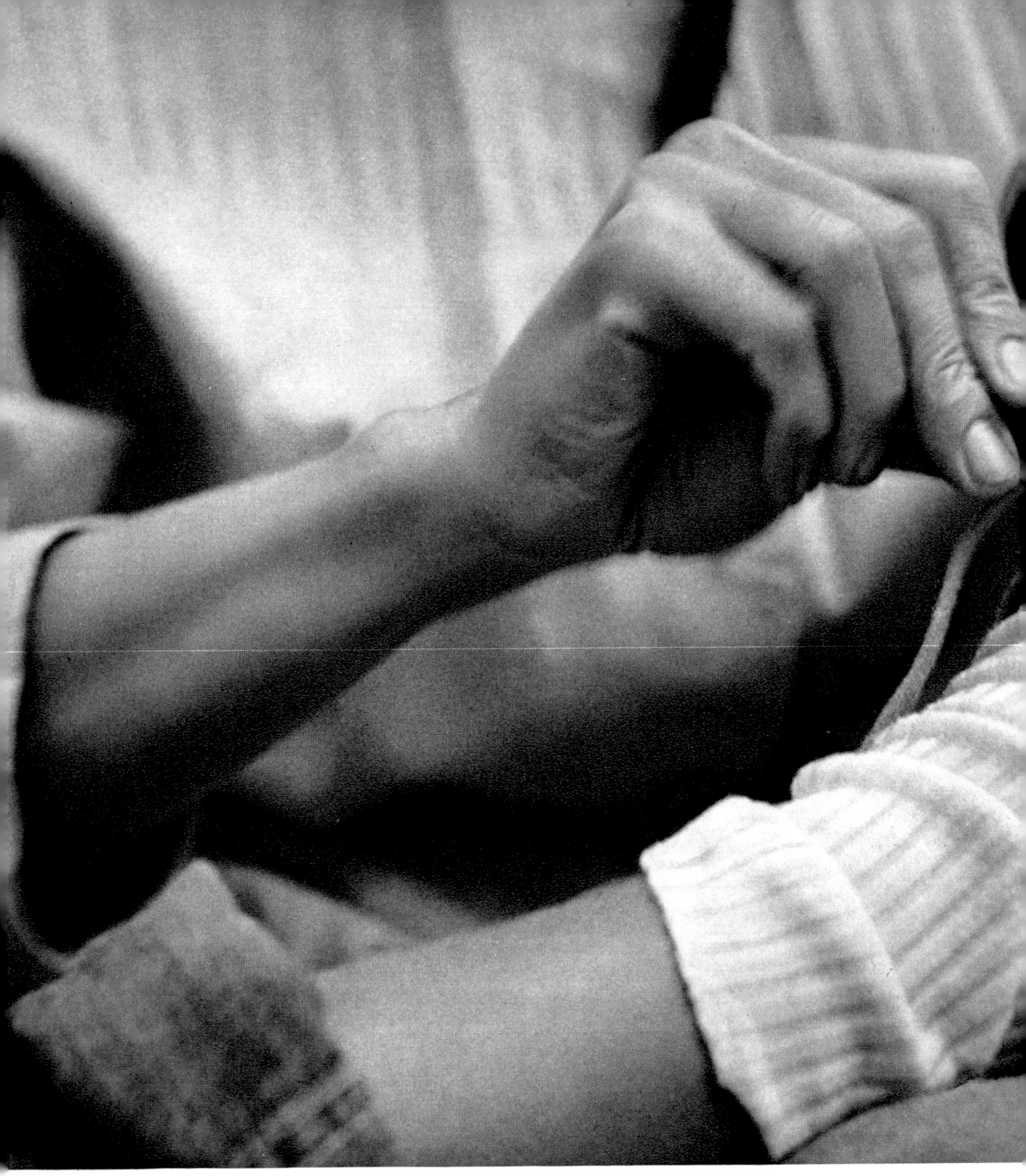

"I'm quite as big for me," said he,
"As you are big for you."

John Kendrick Bangs

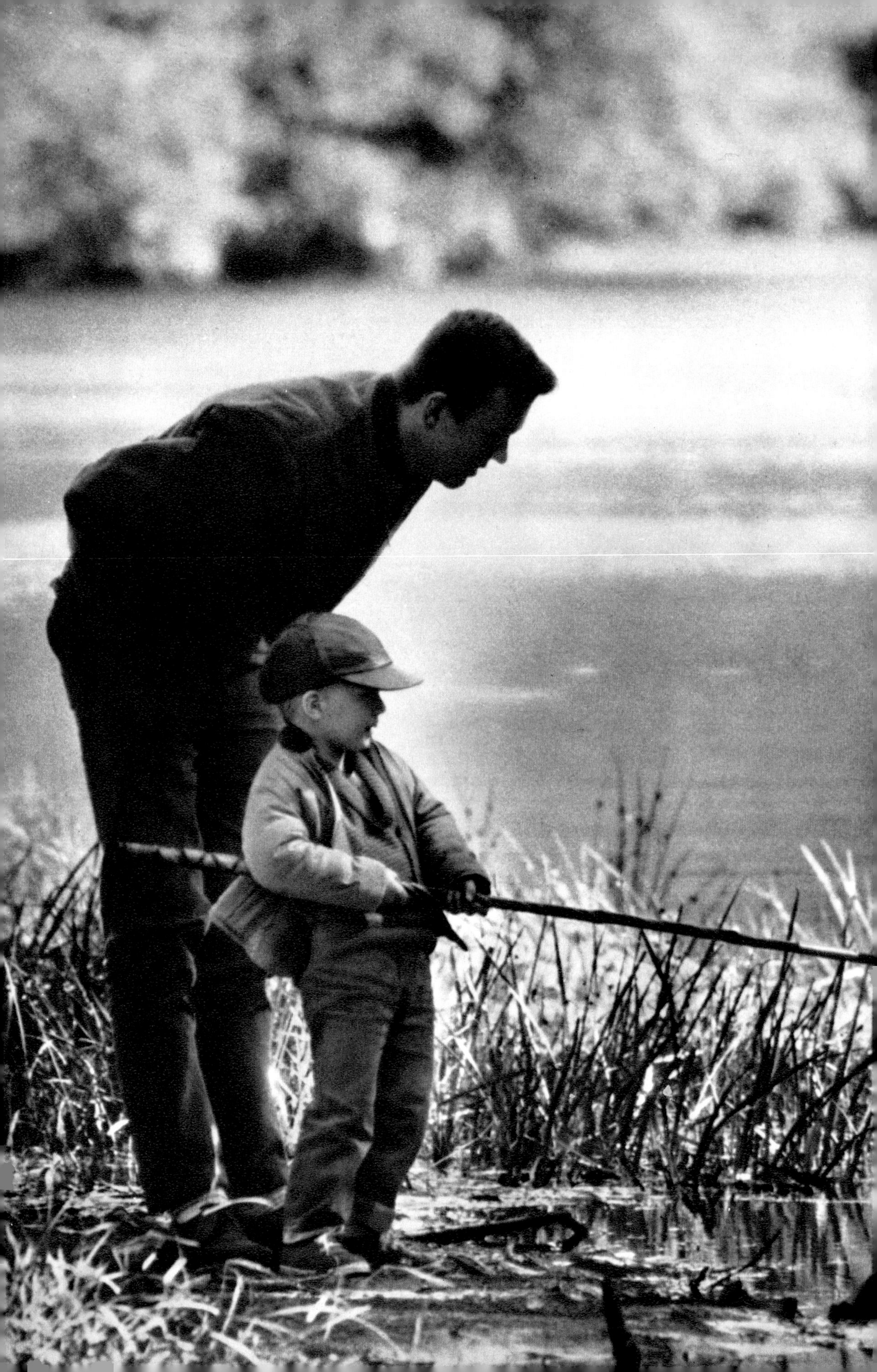

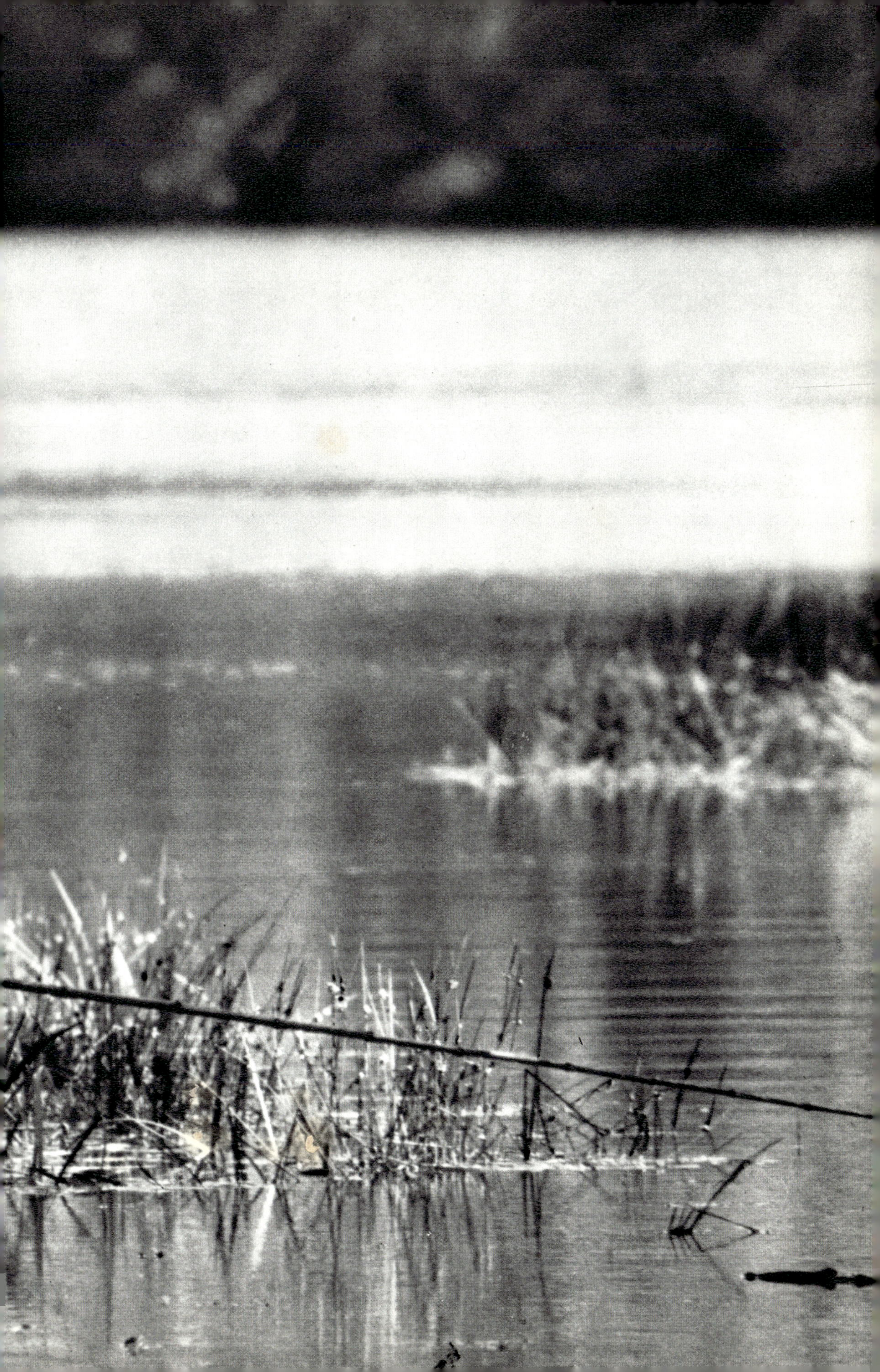

A woman is as old as she looks to a man that likes to look at her.

Finley Peter Dunne

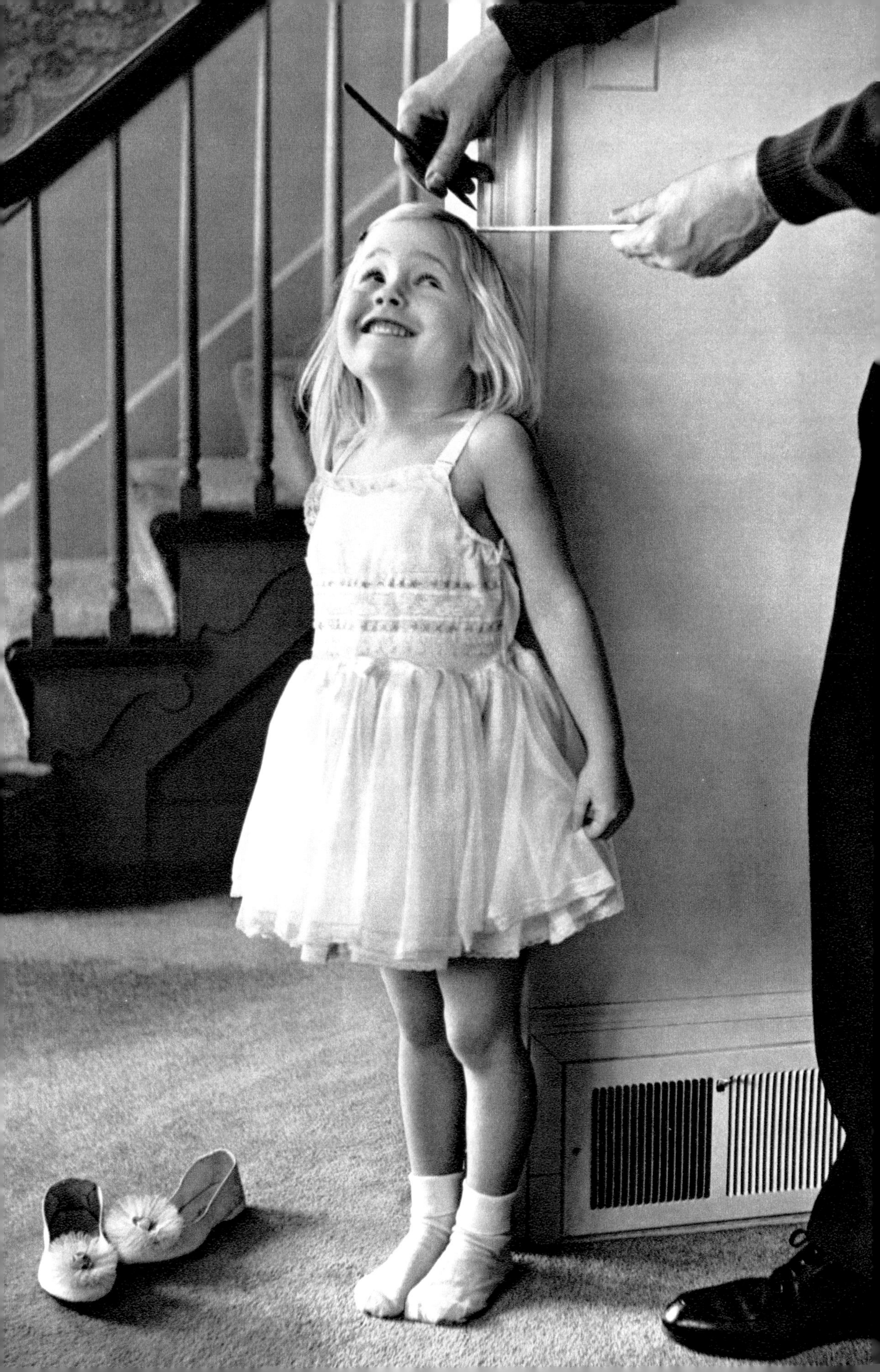

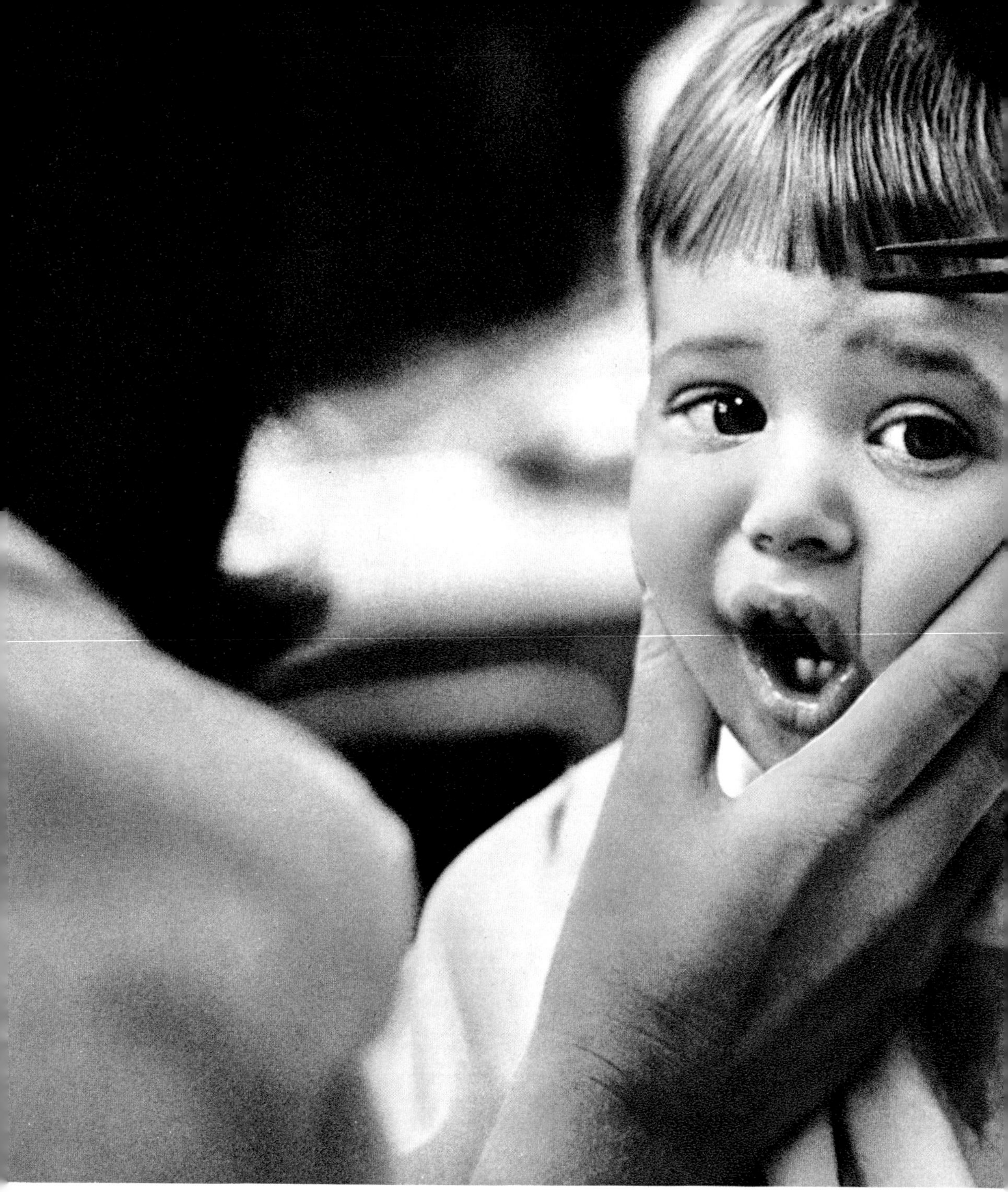

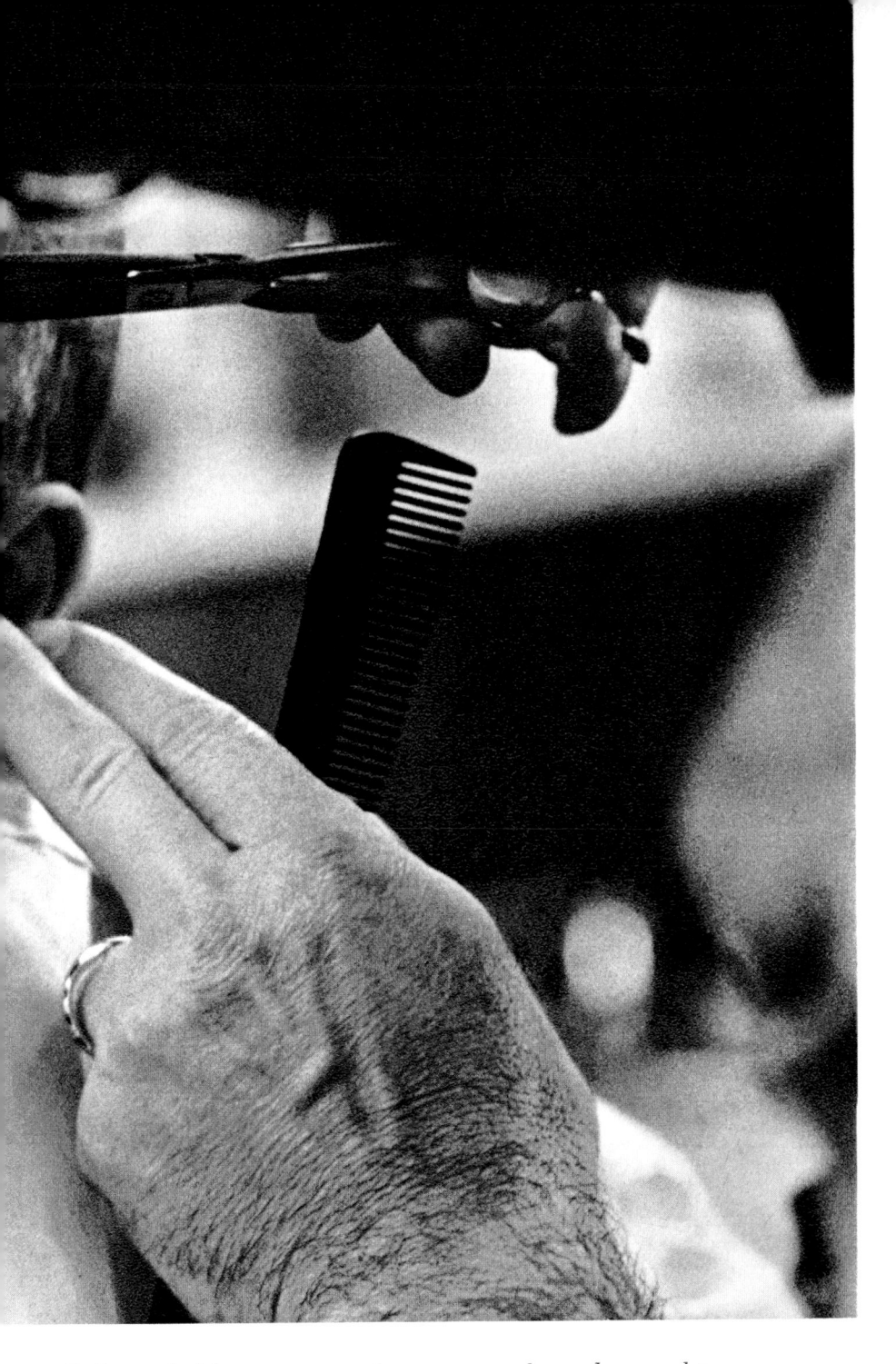

When children are taught not merely to know things but particularly to know themselves, not merely how to do things but particularly how to compel themselves to do things, they may be said to be really educated.

Edwin Grant Conklin

All the duties of religion are eminently solemn and venerable in the eyes of children. But none will so strongly prove the sincerity of the parents; none so powerfully awaken the reverence of the child ... as family devotions, particularly those in which petitions for the children occupy a distinguished place.

Timothy Dwight

A happy family is but an earlier heaven.

Sir John Bowring

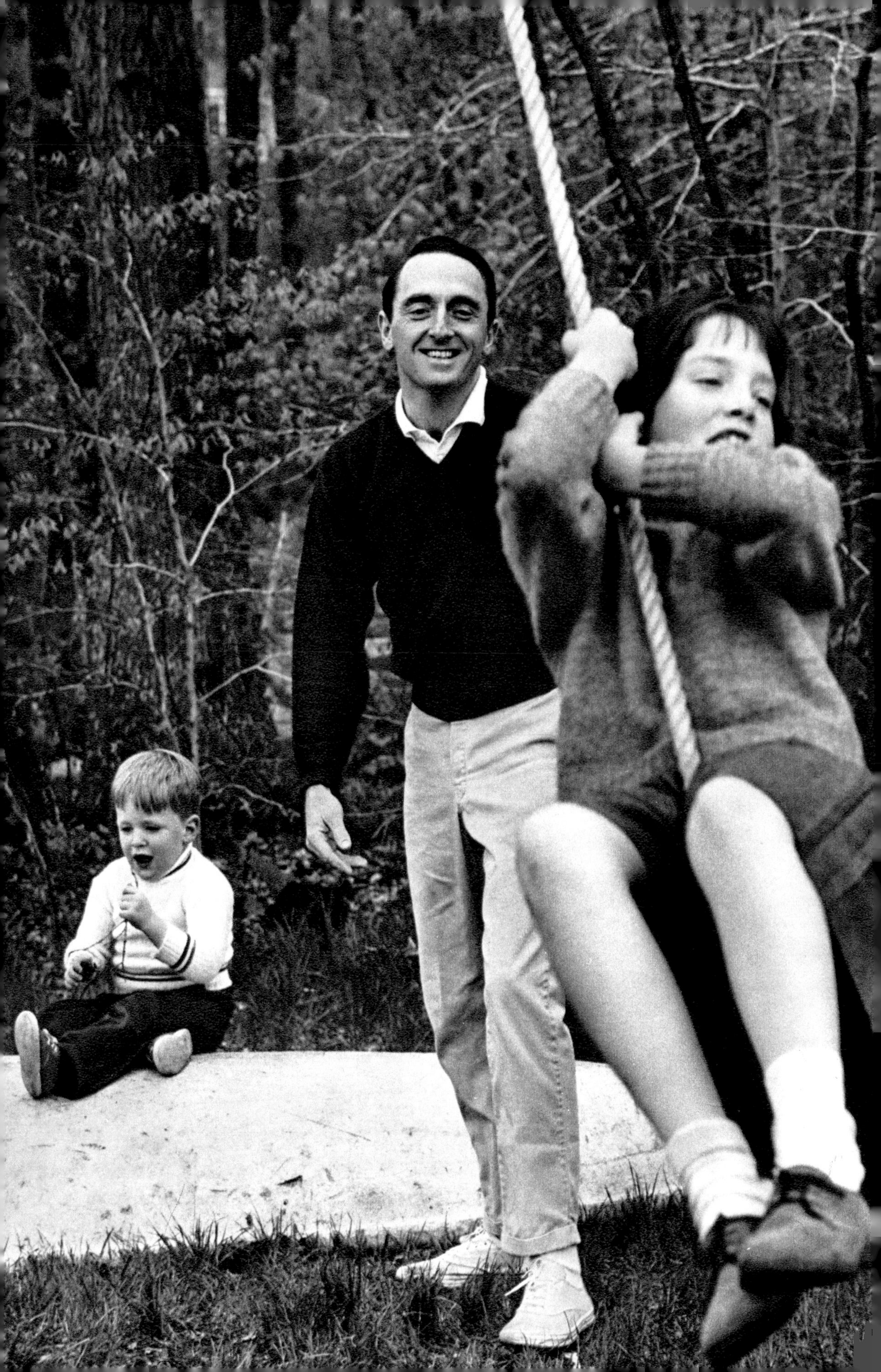

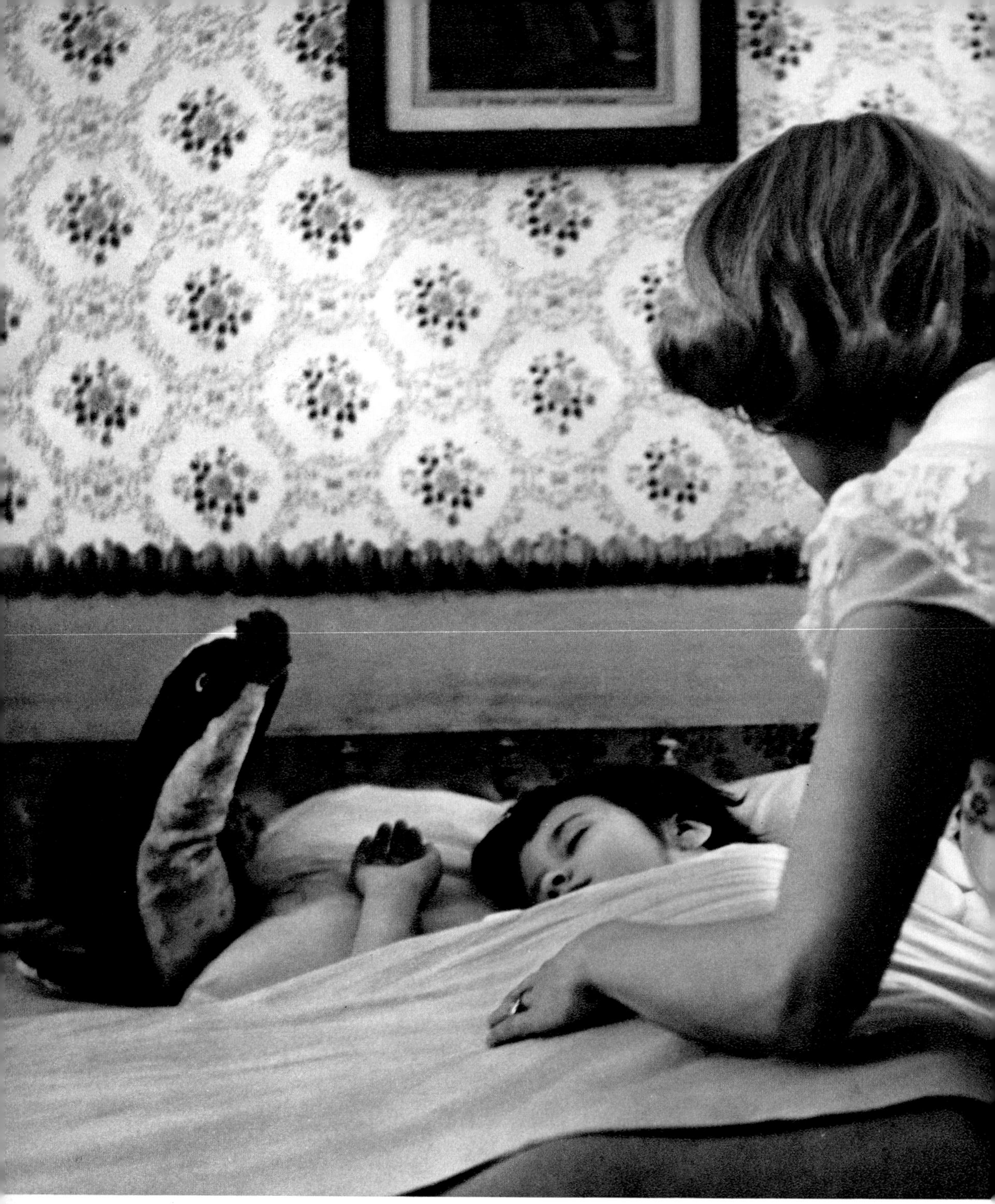

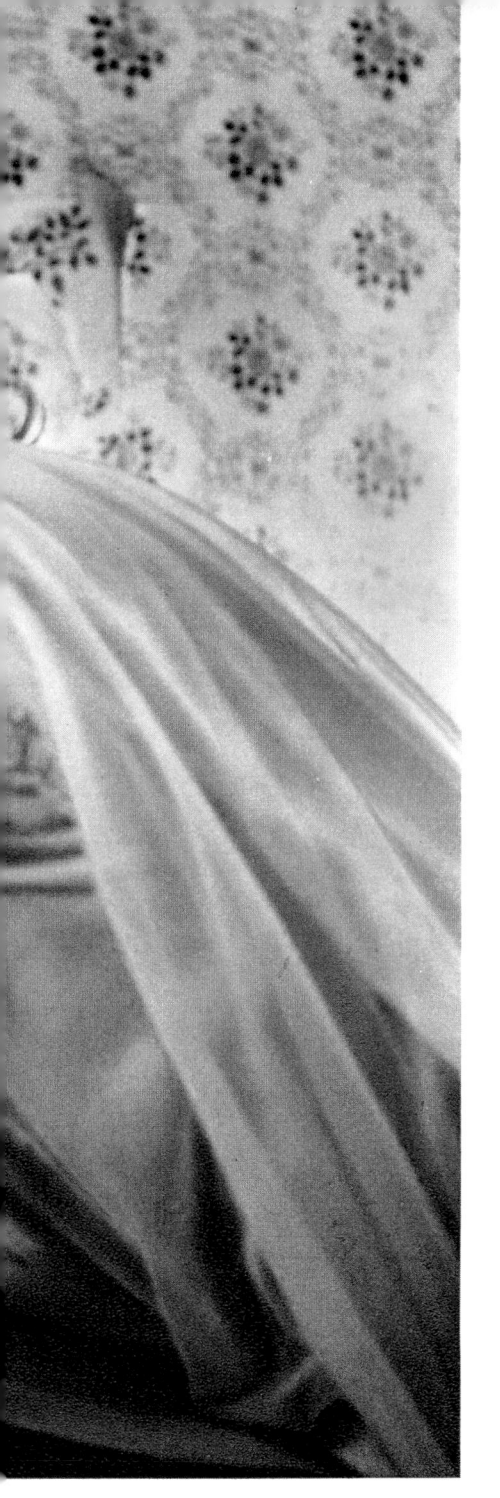

So for the mother's sake the child was dear,
And dearer was the mother for the child.

Samuel Taylor Coleridge

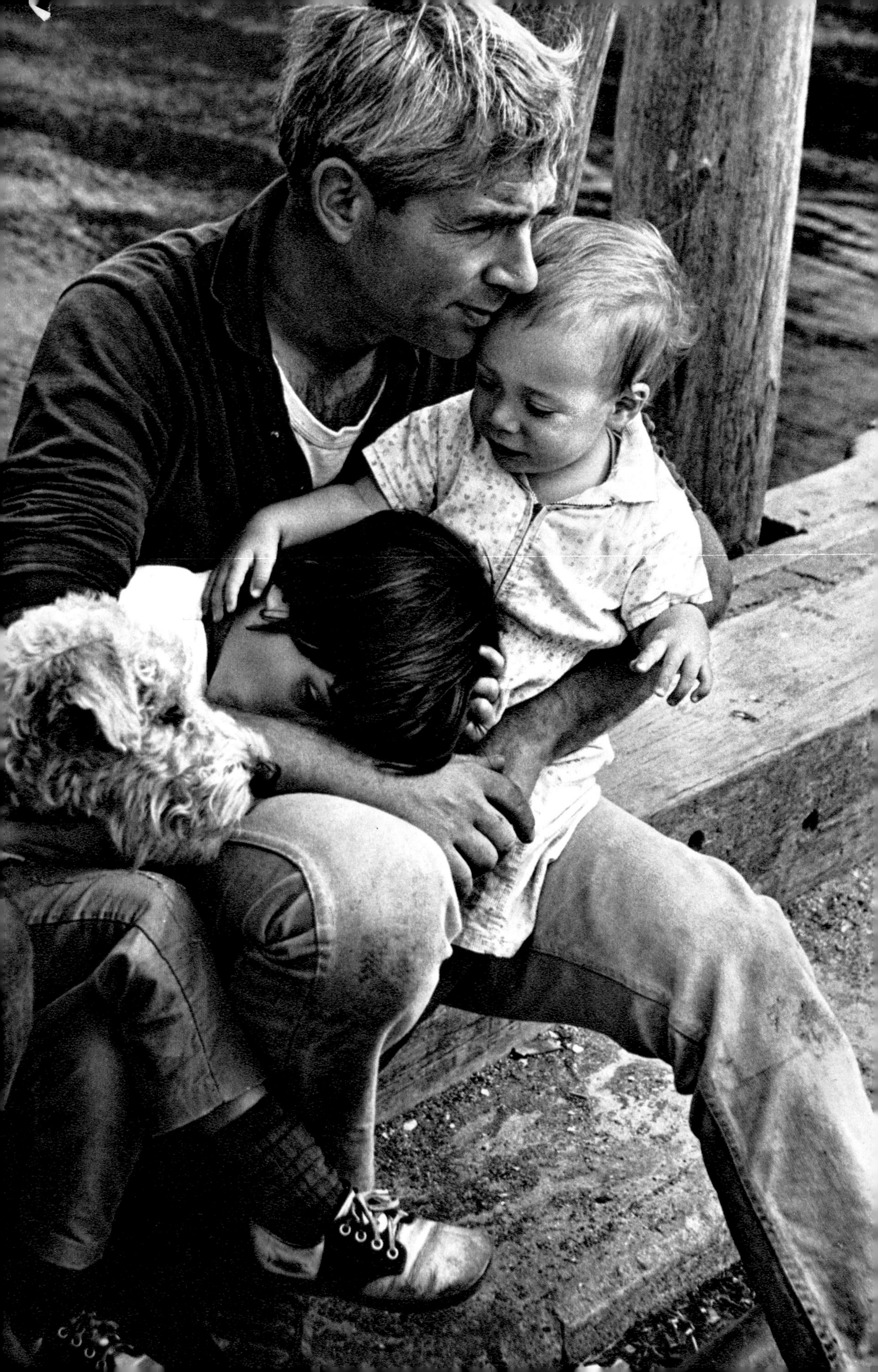

I still find each day too short for all the
thoughts I want to think...

...all the walks I want
to take, all the books I want
to read and all the
friends I want to see.
The longer I live, the
more my mind dwells upon the
beauty and wonder of
the world.

John Burroughs

PHOTO CREDITS—Cover & frontispiece: George Daniell, Photo Researchers • 6-7: Christopher G. Knight, Photo Researchers • 8 top: Charles Harbutt, Magnum • 8 bottom: Bruce Davidson, Magnum • 9: Elliott Erwitt, Magnum • 11: Dwayne Bey, Bethel • 12: Dennis Stock, Magnum • 13: Costa Manos, Magnum • 14: Susan McCartney, Photo Researchers • 15: Grete Mannheim, Photo Researchers • 16: Doris Pinney, Photo-Library • 17: Fritz Henle, Photo Researchers • 18 top: John Rees, Black Star • 18 bottom: Stephen Frisch, Photo Researchers • 19 top: John Rees, Black Star • 19 bottom: Sergio Larrain, Magnum • 20 top: Erika, Photo Researchers • 20 bottom: Bob Lerner, Look Magazine • 21: Eve Arnold, Magnum • 22-23: Erika, Photo Researchers • 24: John Rees, Black Star • 25 top: John Rees, Black Star • 25 bottom: Larry B. Nicholson, Photo Researchers • 27: Fred Lyon, Rapho-Guillumette • 29: Guy Gillette, Photo Researchers • 30-31: Hella Hammid, Rapho-Guillumette • 32: Cornell Capa, Magnum • 33 top: Stern, from Black Star • 33 bottom: Myron Wood, Photo Researchers • 34 top: Bob Lerner, Look Magazine • 34 bottom: John Rees, Black Star • 35: John Rees, Black Star • 37: Fred Lyon, Rapho-Guillumette • 38: Matt Herron, Black Star • 39 top: Wayne Miller, Magnum • 39 bottom: Robert S. Smith, Rapho-Guillumette • 40: Bruce Roberts, Rapho-Guillumette • 41 top: Erika, Photo Researchers • 41 bottom: Jackie Curtis, Photo Researchers • 43: Robert S. Smith, Rapho-Guillumette • 44: Bruce Roberts, Rapho-Guillumette • 45 top: Grete Mannheim, Photo Researchers • 45 bottom: Bruce Roberts, Rapho-Guillumette • 46: Burk Uzzle, Magnum • 47: Eve Arnold, Magnum • 48: Bruce Roberts, Rapho-Guillumette • 49: Charles Harbutt, Magnum • 50: Eve Arnold, Magnum • 53: William Stone, Photo Researchers • 54: Elliott Erwitt, Magnum • 55: C. Robert Lee, Photo Researchers • 56: Sean Kernan, Bethel • 58-59: Elliott Erwitt, Magnum • 60 top: Bruce Roberts, Rapho-Guillumette • 60 bottom: John Rees, Black Star • 61: Michael Sullivan, Black Star • 62 top: Grete Mannheim, Photo Researchers • 62 bottom: John Russell • 63 top: Doris Pinney, Photo-Library • 63 bottom: Esther Henderson, Rapho-Guillumette • 64: Burk Uzzle, Magnum • 65: Bruce Roberts, Rapho-Guillumette • 66 top: Jane Latta, Photo Researchers • 66 bottom: Martha Reker, Photo Researchers • 67: Erika, Photo Researchers • 68: Marion Bernstein, Bethel • 71: Cornell Capa, Magnum • 72: Hella Hammid, Rapho-Guillumette • 73: Archie Liberman, Look Magazine • 74: Matt Herron, Black Star • 75: Fonssagrives, Photo Researchers • 76: Marc & Evelyne Bernheim, Rapho-Guillumette • 77: Ted Spiegel, Bethel • 78: Joe Munroe, Photo Researchers • 79 top: J. W. Cella, Photo Researchers • 79 bottom: Fritz Henle, Photo Researchers • 80: Edward Lettau, Photo Researchers • 82-83: Frederick C. Baldwin, Photo Researchers • 85: Doris Pinney, Photo-Library • 86-87: Don Gettsug, Rapho-Guillumette • 88: John Rees, Black Star • 89: Charles Harbutt, Magnum • 90: Dick Davis, Photo Researchers • 91: Laszlo Hege, Photo Researchers • 92: Marion Bernstein, Bethel • Larry Silverstein, Photo Researchers

Printed and bound by Arnoldo Mondadori, Verona, Italy